Complementing the Welfare State:
The development of private pension,
health insurance and other employee benefits
in the United States

Labour-Management Relations Series No. 65

Complementing the Welfare State: The development of private pension, health insurance and other employee benefits in the United States

Beth Stevens

International Labour Office   Geneva

ISBN 92-2-105673-2
ISSN 0538-8325

First published 1986

Printed by the International Labour Office, Geneva, Switzerland

For most enterprises of any size, pay is much more complex than basic wages. The pay packets regularly received by workers often include a whole series of complementary cash payments, including various forms of performance related and personal qualifications bonuses, cost-of-living allowances, premium pay for hours worked outside the normal pattern and various payments for expenses or inconveniences incurred. In addition to this "direct pay" regularly received for the time spent at work, there is also a host of indirect forms of remuneration, sometimes described as "fringe benefits", or (in recognition of the fact that they are no longer of marginal significance) "employee benefits" or "wage supplements". Although there is an almost infinite variety of benefits, those most frequently used may be grouped under the following categories: (a) pay for time not worked; (b) social security benefits; (c) bonuses and gratuities normally paid at more than monthly intervals; (d) welfare or employee services; (e) housing; and (f) other forms of payment in kind.

In recognition of the fact that indirect remuneration may now account for one-third or more of total labour costs, the ILO has recently begun to look more closely at this important aspect of pay. Thus, various studies of the incidence and forms of indirect remuneration in ASEAN countries were carried out, and their findings discussed in a subregional meeting in Tokyo in December 1983. A more conceptual study on the subject, prepared by H. Zoeteweij, is being published this year under the title Indirect Remuneration: An international overview.

The present case study of the United States documents how various forms of benefits emerged in that country. There has been a tendency to regard most elements of indirect remuneration as being imposed by the State as an unwelcome additional cost to employers. An effort has been made in this research to provide a more accurate historical perspective on the origins of indirect remuneration by tracing how employee benefits have developed over the last century as a pragmatic combination of public and private sector decisions. Indeed, the study argues that where employer-developed benefit programmes are successful alternatives to public sector programmes, they effectively set what may become de facto social policy. By considering a series of compromises, choices and public policy decisions, the study shows how employer-sponsored benefit programmes finally proved to be the most successful private sector response to meeting workers' needs. Other attempts at developing such programmes which did not meet with ultimate success were made by various ethnic groups, community associations, charitable fraternal societies and trade unions.

This historical study concentrates on health insurance and pension schemes in the United States and shows how, in an area characterised by often heated debate between partisans of "human needs" and "economic efficiency", employee benefits may be seen as a successful area of compromise solutions in that, while constituting social welfare payments, they remain an important form of compensation in the effort-reward relationship between employers and employees. As a result, the types of benefits offered are subject to business considerations as well as to humanitarian or social policy concerns. Employee benefits have emerged as an important subject of collective bargaining, and the study shows how the attitudes of trade unions towards this form of pay have evolved over the years. It is argued that the ultimate success of employee benefit programmes as they have developed in the United States lies in the fact that they have met the needs of both employers and trade unions and attracted the timely support of federal policy-makers.

The book starts with an introductory chapter on the general nature of employee benefits as they have developed in the United States. Chapter II traces the development of private sector benefits from their beginnings in the nineteenth century to the dramatic expansion in collective bargaining over benefits that took place in the 1940s. Chapter III traces this history from the 1940s to the 1970s, focusing on variations in the spread of benefits across different employers and types of employees. Chapter IV considers the same period, this time concentrating on the changes that occurred in the substantive content of the benefits adopted. The fifth and final chapter summarises the major features of the growth of private sector benefits with a view to offering an explanation of the factors that have helped to shape the development of the private side of the welfare state.

This book is a condensed version of a study prepared by Beth Stevens in 1983, under a joint programme of research between the ILO and Boston University, United States.

CONTENTS

List of tables

CHAPTER I

THE DUAL NATURE OF EMPLOYEE BENEFITS

Half-way between a reward and a right, employee benefits represent a compromise between social obligations and private means. Seen from one perspective, they are rewards for work, simple alternatives to wages. They merely come in the form of pensions, holidays with pay and various types of insurance. Seen from another perspective they are both private sector substitutes for and supplements to public sector programmes: national health insurance, social security and workers' compensation.

Benefits as a part of the welfare state

The development of this hybrid social institution has been part of a broader transformation of the ways in which economic resources are distributed by society. Over the past century, one of the more pervasive social changes in industrialised nations has been the shift from the distribution of economic resources through the market to a mixed system where wages and socially insured benefits are distributed by both the market and public institutions. This shift, often termed the growth of the "welfare state", has altered the ways in which individuals are assured of economic security. The traditional choice between work or private charity has been replaced by a varied set of government-supported stipends and employer-sponsored services that supplement wages. Individuals now receive varying combinations of services and programmes such as family allowances, pensions, medical care and disability insurance. Gradually, these resources have become a substantial part of the economies of industrialised societies. By 1975 the proportion of the gross national product devoted to such public and private social transfer programmes ranged from 10.2 per cent in Switzerland to a full 26 per cent in the Netherlands, with the remaining industrialised countries falling in between.

Most of the attention paid to this transformation, however, has been on the role played by the public sector. The common view of the welfare state, particularly in the United States, has been one of government provision of funds and services. Public discussion about the advantages and disadvantages of welfare state programmes have concerned the public programmes of social security (the national system of old-age, survivors' and disability insurance), aid to families with dependent children (AFDC) and Medicare. When looking at other societies, Americans have focused on the national health service in the United Kingdom or the reportedly "cradle to grave" social welfare systems of Scandinavia. The debate has been about bureaucracies versus markets, rational planning versus the laws of supply and demand, possession based on rights versus possession based on economic resources. Amidst this debate most Americans have failed to perceive the paradox of market institutions that distribute benefits that moderate market forces in the same ways as public institutions do. Few people have paid attention to the "private side of the welfare state".

In fact, social welfare programmes have never been solely the product of public institutions. Most welfare state societies distribute social welfare benefits through a variety of channels. While old-age pensions, family allowances or health-care benefits are in some societies distributed by the Government, in other societies private sector institutions have taken on the task. Indeed, private corporate or employer-based non-monetary remuneration has become an important segment of total social welfare expenditures. This is particularly true for the United States. American society is distinctly characterised by the use of the private sector to provide economic security. In 1975, non-public institutions were responsible for over one-quarter of the social welfare expenditures in this country.[1] Non-governmental social welfare programmes pay for one-fifth of the income maintenance programmes and over half of health insurance expenditures.[2]

One major and ever-increasing part of non-governmental welfare expenditures is provided by employers in the form of payments and services to employees and their families. Cross-national data on the extent of such expenditures are sketchy at best. One study however has estimated that the proportion of total labour costs devoted to "other labour costs", i.e. non-wage benefits, range from 46 per cent in Italy to 16 per cent in Denmark, with the United States private sector devoting approximately 26 per cent of labour costs to such expenditures.[3]

This lack of recognition of the important role of employee benefits has had several consequences. First, it has clouded the perceptions of the factors that influenced the development of the public sector programmes whose existence has been so greatly debated. The development of public sector programmes, such as social security, cannot be fully understood without recognising the role played by the private pension system as both an alternative and a supplement. Where they are alternatives, employer-developed benefits set de facto social policy. Employer choices concerning the purchase of health insurance, for example, determine the limits of medical treatment for approximately 85 per cent of the American population under 65 years of age. Since health insurance determines which treatment will be reimbursed, it effectively defines which treatment will be used by patients and physicians.[4] Employer rules on the age at which workers can qualify for retirement pensions have an impact on the labour force participation of older workers.

2

Where fringe benefits act as supplements to government programmes, they serve as pressure valves and regulate demands on public sector programmes. Pensions that provide inadequate benefits, for example, result in increased pressure on the political system to raise social security benefits. Whether as substitutes or supplements, private benefits programmes by their very existence become entrenched institutional arrangements. Particularly if they are widespread, they can become a road-block to public sector attempts to provide similar social welfare benefits.

Secondly, this slow recognition of the important role played by fringe benefits has led to ignoring a social institution that encapsulates within itself many of the issues historically under debate in American politics. Employee benefits have been created in an era that has been host to a major debate between two camps holding conflicting views. Concepts of human need have clashed with concepts of financial efficiency. Questions of the rights of individuals to financial security have had to be posed next to questions of the appropriateness of bringing non-economic considerations into a market institution. The supporters and critics of employee benefits have marshalled arguments that reflect widely different approaches to political and economic issues. Liberals have long favoured the goals of reducing inequalities in income and mitigating the insecurity in life brought about by the market through programmes that transfer income from one group to another. Conservatives, in contrast, have stressed the reduction of social planning programmes that interfere with the market; instead, they favour the greater use of market mechanisms to increase opportunities for advancement and personal saving. Employee benefits are important objects of study because they are a compromise solution. They are market institutions that sponsor programmes based partly on family circumstances and partly on contributions to the firm. They therefore combine some of the precepts of both parties to the larger debate.

Benefits as a reward for work

Employee benefits are only in part a social welfare payment, however. They are also partly remuneration, a component of the employer and the employee relationship. The study of benefits therefore is not just an investigation into the development of a lesser-known part of the welfare state, but is also an exploration into the ways in which the rewards for work are created and distributed.

As a reward for work, rather than a citizenship right, benefits have inevitably become part and parcel of two sets of dynamics. In part they become one more component of labour costs, joining wages and recruitment expenses as part of the cost of maintaining a workforce. And in part they become caught up in the battle for control over the workplace.

For employers, benefits are part of the cost of doing business. They purchase health insurance policies, annuities and disability insurance combinations in the same way as they purchase casualty insurance to guard against damage to the manufacturing plant. This approach has ramifications for the development of benefits, however. For employers, the content and scope of benefits are financial matters as well as types of protection. Decisions about the provision of a benefits programme determines the cost of benefits and through this the cost of labour. Different types of benefits cost varying amounts: health insurance is frequently used and thus is expensive, but long-term disability insurance is not; pensions require large amounts of advance funding, but profit-sharing plans work on a yearly basis. In sum, different choices result in different financial pressures. These in turn affect plans for expansion, productivity rates and profit ratios. Thus the types of benefits offered, as well as their internal provisions, are subject to business considerations as well as to humanitarian or social policy concerns.

Benefits are also "tools", tools to be used to manipulate employment policies. They can be used to attract certain kinds of labour, retain others or cushion lay-offs. Benefits are used to inspire loyalty and discourage labour turnover.[5] Trade unions, too, deal with benefits as a labour cost. For unions, benefits are additional forms of remuneration that can be obtained through collective bargaining. They give union negotiators more flexibility in satisfying a variety of worker needs and then balancing that with costs to the employers.

Focusing on benefits as part of the welfare state encourages them to be seen as a coherent programme, or as a piece of legislation. Viewing benefits as a labour cost highlights their variation. Different employers and unions face different types of labour markets, command different levels of economic and political resources, and face different regulatory constraints. The study of private sector welfare expenditure then becomes an exploration of the creation of many individual social welfare programmes under widely varying sets of conditions.

The second implication of the fact that benefits are also rewards for work is that benefits inevitably become bound up with the struggle for control over the workplace. For employers, benefits are part of a strategy intended to reduce the appeal of trade unions and thus retain unilateral control over the workplace. For unions, benefits are sometimes the sophisticated descendants of employer paternalism that for years were used to manipulate workers. On the other hand, unions use benefits as countermeasures to employer actions. Union-obtained benefits serve as attractions for unorganised workers and as ways to strengthen loyalty to the union.[6] Thus the development of benefits is a battleground between management and labour for the loyalties of workers at the same time as it is a positive attempt to mitigate the insecurities faced by workers in modern society. Private sector employee benefits thus stand at the

4   6276d

nexus of two critical social developments, the growth of the welfare state and the shifting struggle for the power to determine the rewards for work.

The research study

Despite the important nature of benefits we know little about how social welfare benefits are developed and provided under private auspices. Unlike government programmes, where the motives and interests behind decisions to allocate resources are relatively public and well understood, the factors and interests behind the creation of private sector benefits are lost in a welter of unilateral corporate decisions, complex labour negotiations, the marketing tactics of insurers, and the rulings of federal and state agencies. We need to understand the ways in which social welfare concerns are combined with private sector considerations of labour cost and labour control.

If this society is going to depend on its social welfare needs being met through such a mixed system, we must understand the philosophies and constraints that shaped those programmes.

The purpose of this research is to trace the development of employee benefits in the United States over the last century, in order to begin to explore this intersection between public and private sector practices. The research will particularly focus on the last 40 years, however; this time span covers the period in which the bulk of benefits were created and then diffused across the American economy. In this report, an attempt will be made to uncover the reasons why benefits have taken on the specific form found today. American society has chosen to develop a private welfare system where employers offer protection to their workers (and those individuals with a legal tie to workers), usually in the form of insurance, against various forms of catastrophes or financial insecurity. There are a host of choices that have been made in the construction of that system. There was nothing inevitable about it. Other modern industrialised nations have taken different paths of development. This study will trace the development of the system of private sector employee benefits in order to identify the specific political, economic and organisational factors that have led to this peculiarly American form of the welfare state.

Notes

[1] Alfred Skolnick and Sophie Dales: "Social welfare expenditures 1950-75", in Social Security Bulletin (Washington, DC, United States Social Security Administration), 1976, No. 39, pp. 3-20.

[2] Hugh Mosley: Public and private social welfare systems: A working paper on the underdevelopment of state social welfare institutions in the US (Berlin (West), International

Institute for Comparative Social Research, Wissenschaftszentrum, 1978).

[3] Martin Rein: "The social policy of the firm", in Policy Sciences (Amsterdam, Elsevier Scientific Publishing Co.), 1982, No. 1, pp. 1-18.

[4] Walter Kolodrubetz: "Group health insurance coverage of full-time employees, 1972", in Social Security Bulletin (Washington, DC, United States Social Security Administration), 1974, No. 37.

[5] Fred Foulkes: Personnel policies in large non-union companies (Englewood Cliffs, New Jersey, Prentice-Hall, 1980); Bradley Schiller and Robert Weiss: "The impact of private pensions on firm attachment", in Review of Economics and Statistics (Harvard University), 1979, No. 61, pp. 369-380.

[6] Thomas Kochan: Collective bargaining and industrial relations (Homewood, Illinois, Richard D. Unwin Inc., 1980).

CHAPTER II

THE SEARCH FOR SOLUTIONS:
FRINGE BENEFITS TO 1950

The reward for work has seldom been solely in the form of cold hard cash. From turkeys at Christmas to privileges at the company store, employers have long enumerated workers with non-monetary benefits as well. This century, however, has transformed non-wage benefits into sophisticated programmes barely related to the old paternalistic practices. Since 1900 non-wage remuneration has expanded from benefits "in kind" that address simple physical needs to complex financial instruments that bolster the long-term financial security of workers. The development of these instruments such as pensions, life and health insurance and long-term disability payments (LTD plans) has made for a decided change in the way employers remunerate employees. In turn, these changes have transformed the ties that bind workers and employers together. By requiring long-term commitments of funding and disbursement to workers, such benefits have strengthened the ties that bind employees to the firm, creating financial exchanges that continue for decades. By providing large financial settlements, employers became entwined in the affairs of their employees' beneficiaries, becoming progressively involved in defining family relations. And by offering complex financial rewards for work, employers were led into developing a system of counsellors, administrators and adjudicators that provide those benefits. The result of all these changes has been the establishment of an extensive system of private sector activities that serve in part as both a substitute for and a supplement to government programmes that ensure the security of citizens.

The century before 1950 saw the development, and often demise, of a variety of private sector institutions intended to provide group-based solutions to the problems of financial insecurity. These efforts took diverse forms ranging from direct provision of care to relief funds and group insurance. They can be divided into four major categories defined by the major sponsors involved: ethnic and fraternal organisation plans, union-sponsored benefits, employee mutual relief funds and employer-sponsored benefit plans.

Ethnic and fraternal society benefits programmes

The first known instance of sharing the cost of illness came in 1778 when the Free African Society of Philadelphia set up a relief fund for its members. This was followed in the early and mid-1800s by additional Negro "benevolent" societies, benevolent societies run by the French and German communities, and "centros", local clubs run by Hispanic groups in Florida. All offered either direct provision of care, or the replacement of income lost due to sickness. Most of these ethnically based societies remained fairly small and never protected large segments of the American population. Based on ethnic and local ties, they did not have the scope to develop funds sufficient to withstand long periods of heavy utilisation, or economic depression when membership withered.

Other social ties also formed the basis for a communal solution to life crises. From the late 1860s to the early 1920s, "fraternal societies", such as the Odd Fellows or the Lions, offered death, pension and sickness benefits to their members. Some were non-sectarian, charitable organisations that offered insurance to non-members as a sideline to their fund-raising and social activities; others were solely devoted to providing low-cost benefits to community members. Since their dues were cheaper than regular life insurance premiums, they prospered for the first few decades. Fraternal insurance appealed to the middle class that had little access to the early union funds. By 1917 just short of half of all insured lives in the United States were insured by fraternal societies, but by 1927 fraternal societies had gone into rapid decline. The reasons were not hard to find. Most of these societies kept little or no reserves, since they were not as strictly regulated as regular insurance companies. Since their benefits were drawn from the payment of dues by current members, they had to rely on a constant volume of membership in order to provide benefits. This sufficed in the early years, but as the members grew older they increasingly made claims for sickness, pension or burial payments. Without adequate reserves, the mutual benefit societies had no resources to handle the rise in claims. The funds had to enrol more and more members or raise dues in order to cover larger expenses. But as dues grew more expensive, fewer people became members and increasing numbers of societies went bankrupt. By the 1920s, most of their potential members had ceased to join the fraternal societies and began to purchase regular life insurance.[1] A few of the remaining fraternal societies tried to reorganise their funds so as to become actuarially responsible (i.e. keep reserves like insurance companies) but the damage had been done. Fraternal societies were no longer seen as the solution to financial insecurity.

Union-sponsored benefits programmes

Occupational benevolent societies provided a more enduring form of group-based protection. In 1806 the Journeyman Cabinetmakers formed a benevolent society, followed by the Philadelphia Typographical Society in 1810. These mutual aid societies offered loans and burial assistance. Such societies often formed the basis for trade unions. In 1829 the Journeyman Cabinetmakers took on "industrial functions" in order to "endeavour to settle all disputes arising between them and their employers".[2] The Iron Molders and Locomotive Engineers benevolent societies followed the same path 40 years later going from aid society to trade unions. This pattern was repeated in a number of other occupations and industries; repeated so often in fact that it seemed that "trade unionism in America rose as much from a desire to band together for mutual insurance as from a desire to bargain collectively".[3]

Trade unions, whether or not they began as benevolent societies, began to use various benefits as organising tools beginning in the 1850s. Benefits were seen as increasing the retention of membership. Samuel Gompers, an early leader of the labour movement, saw benefits as a tie that bound workers to the union. He argued that members would be less likely to drop out of the union if that meant losing access to union benefits. Such benefits were obviously unilateral plans, funded and administered by the unions. Unions had no intention of sharing the credit with employers.

The earliest union cash benefits were for sickness. The first programme was set up by the Granite Cutters' Union in 1877; in the next two decades the Barbers', Tobacco Workers' and Printers' Unions followed suit. By 1904, 28 of the 117 member unions of the American Federation of Labor (AFL) had sickness benefit plans. Pensions came later, with the Granite Cutters leading the way in 1905. By 1928, 40 per cent of union members were in unions that had pension plans.[4] Ten unions had pension programmes with 11,000 annuitants receiving pensions.

Meanwhile, unions also took a more active role in ensuring the financial security of workers, by directly providing services to their members. The International Ladies Garment Workers' Union (LLGWU) and the Amalgamated Clothing Workers established medical clinics, originally in order to aid them in the administration of their sickness benefits programmes, by providing (or confirming) diagnoses and thus preventing fraudulent claims. Later the union expanded the clinics to offer diagnostic services to members under all circumstances. Other unions, rather than providing pensions, built retirement homes or tuberculosis sanatoriums.[5] Still others, responding to the growth of insurance benefits by employers established by their own insurance companies. Two of the more successful companies were the Union Cooperative Insurance Association formed by the International Brotherhood of Electrical Workers (IBEW) and the Union Labor Life Insurance Company established by the AFL in 1928. All told, by 1927, a government survey found that 73 international unions were paying out a range of benefits totalling nearly US$28 million. This total underestimates the actual benefits disbursed by the labour movement, as it does not include the myriad of smaller programmes run by local unions.

Yet, a downturn had already begun by the early years of this century. The number of unions paying sickness benefits had declined by more than 50 per cent between 1903 and 1923. The same survey reporting that unions had paid out US$28 million in benefits in 1927 also admitted that "a gradually evolving tendency appears to be the shifting of the responsibility for certain conditions on to the employers".[6] By 1938, only ten years later, the majority of unions were dispensing only US$25 million in benefits. Trade union benefits never became the dominant institution for the protection of workers from the calamities of old age, sickness and death.

This failure to establish a unilateral union benefits system can be traced to several sources, not the least of which was the labour movement's own ambivalence towards benefits. Despite an early sociological verdict that unions were excellent sponsors of sickness benefits and health insurance, the attitudes of unions toward benefits programmes fluctuated widely. While Samuel Gompers applauded the usefulness of benefits, other union leaders deplored them as a constant source of trouble.[7] From the 1820s to the 1940s, the union movement was torn between an awareness of the advantages and moral credit attached to the practice of helping their members and an awareness of the numerous costs that it entailed.

The advantages to unions of providing benefits were clear. They attracted members, particularly when benefits were not easily available through other channels. They helped to solidify that support into loyalty. They filled an obvious need for protection of their members by providing a bulwark against financial disaster. They also served as a force to prop up wages. By giving older workers sickness and out-of-work benefits, unions kept more vulnerable members from taking non-union jobs and lowering the wage rate.

The disadvantages to unions are less obvious but more complex. First, since union benefits had to be financed by assessments from members, union dues went up as benefits funds were used more often or as they became more adequate. These increases were usually unpopular. This unpopularity kept union benefits at a low level. In 1905 unions provided weekly sickness benefits ranging from US$3 to US$5.25. By 1943, almost 40 years later, the weekly rates provided by the six remaining national plans ranged from US$4 to US$10 (with four of those plans at the US$4 and US$5 level). By that time labour union benefits were lower than benefits paid by either mutual benefit associations or group insurance policies. Pensions were even more difficult for unions to finance. The constantly rising costs, as more members reached retirement age, placed a great burden on unions. This limited pensions plans to all but the largest and most prosperous of them.

Second, benefits funds were tremendously vulnerable during economic downturns. During such periods fewer members could afford the dues, while at the same time more members were making larger claims for benefits. And third, benefits often forced the union to pay a price in internal solidarity. Most unions became caught up on the horns of a difficult dilemma: they could approve most claims for benefits thereby draining the funds and pushing up dues, or they could apply stringent standards and deny claims, thereby alienating members.

All of these constraints caused most unions to regard benefits with a good deal of ambivalence. This ambivalence was not the sole cause of their failure to establish a labour-based benefits system, however. Problems in the design and implementation of benefits were another factor in this lack of success. Most union benefits funds were not funded according to actuarial principles; they generally had few reserves and no systematic estimates of utilisation and costs. Furthermore, unions often drew on the sickness or death benefit funds for general union purposes, so payments were unreliable and financing was shaky. Funds were often poorly administered or were too generous in allowing claims.[8] The difficult economic and political conditions of the 1920s and 1930s dealt the final blow to union hopes. During the 1920s union benefits programmes suffered from the gradual weakening of the labour movement. Membership in unions declined every year from 1920 to 1933. Moreover, the 1920s were a time of rising anti-union sentiment with a number of set-backs in the courts and in Congress.[9] Economic conditions worsened after the crash of 1929 and it became increasingly difficult for unions to collect the dues that supported the benefits. Not only were union members less able to afford the dues but there were fewer members. By the end of the Depression most union pension plans had completely collapsed.

Employee mutual benefit associations

At the same time that unions were sponsoring benefits programmes, a set of organisations, known either as employee benefit associations or mutual relief funds, were developing as an alternative to union plans. Unlike union plans, however, these organisations were specific to individual firms; they did not extend beyond the company. Like union programmes and fraternal societies, employee mutual benefit associations provided forms of aid that minimised the difficulties resulting from illness, accidents and death.

"Relief funds" as they were called by the Commissioner of Labor in 1908, began to develop in the 1860s. Many were organised between 1881 and 1910. By 1908, 750,000 employees worked in establishments that had such funds and 342,000 workers were actually members.

The sponsorship of these organisations varied: workers themselves managed the largest proportion (74 per cent), while 19 per cent were jointly managed by workers and management, and 7 per cent were completely run by the company. Even when managed by the workers, however, the associations had contacts with the employers. In a 1981 survey, 63 per cent of the firms

6276d   11 surveyed reported that they contributed to the funds. (Thirteen per cent of this group did so in only a minor way, such as giving office space, providing clerical assistance or helping to found the organisation.)

Most of these associations were small organisations that primarily offered cash payments to their members to cover burial expenses or lost income due to temporary disabilities. Some employee mutual benefit associations did provide direct services (primarily medical services) to their members. The railway industry was a pioneer in this, with the Southern Pacific Railroad establishing a mutual benefit association offering both cash benefits and medical care in 1868. They were followed by the Missouri Pacific in 1872 and the Northern Pacific in 1882. By 1903, such funds covered 360,000 out of 1.3 million workers. These direct service programmes were often instituted by firms in isolated areas or in hazardous industries. They hired physicians and provided basic medical care to employees and their families.

Despite these successes, employee benefits associations never expanded beyond the level of minor financial assistance. Most remained distributors of small cash benefits, scattered about in individual firms. The very nature of such societies limited their utility. Confined to the employees of one firm, they simply could not spread the costs of claims widely enough to establish a stable financial base. As with union programmes, few employee associations were designed according to actuarial principles; funding was primarily based on dues. The unstable financial base and limited size of these organisations made them unable to offer adequate benefits at an affordable rate.

Employee benefits associations also were limited in their appeal to workers. Because they were voluntary organisations, workers could and did remain non-participants. The clearest limitation in the appeal of employee mutual benefit associations was in their lack of ability to attract the type of workers that needed their services the most. Those workers who were most likely to benefit from the fund – the lowest-paid workers – were the ones least likely to be able to spare the money for dues. Participation in an association varied with its sponsorship. In associations run by fellow employees an average of 30 per cent of the firm's employees were members; in company-sponsored associations an average of 75 per cent of the employees were members. Whether this was due to better advertisement of the association, a feeling that the association would be more stable and thus likely to provide benefits, or whether the benefits were slightly higher if the employer sponsored the group, is not clear. Unfortunately, most benefit associations were run by employees and not management and so overall participation was low. This limitation was the source of the association's ultimate failure. They could not support a major part of their purported constituency.

Thus, the expansion of employee benefits associations or relief funds, like union-sponsored benefit plans, reached a standstill by the late 1930s.   Those associations that continue to exist were gradually transformed into employer-sponsored insured benefits plans.   They still served a purpose, however; they primed the taste of employees for various non-wage benefits.

Employer-sponsored benefits

Employers did not respond to their employees' needs simply by tolerating worker benefits associations.   Employers also developed, although in fits and starts, programmes that provided cash payments and direct services to employees.   Several factors pushed or encouraged employers to begin to provide benefits. Employers developed benefits not only out of the altruistic motive of aiding the unfortunate, but out of what the New York Times in 1913 called "enlightened selfishness".[10]   They responded to four basic sets of events: the rise of labour unrest that led to the appearance of unions, a tightening of the labour market, the disappearance of legal barriers to the formation of group insurance policies and the establishment of legal protections for benefits plans.   The development of group insurance provided a reasonable response to these events; and employer-sponsored benefits became the predominant means for ensuring the financial security of workers.

The first formal benefits sponsored by employers were pension plans.   In 1875, the American Express Company set up the first pension plan in the private sector.   Many railway companies and the Carnegie Steel Company followed with the establishment of pension plans at the end of the century.   These early pensions, however, were no more stable than union plans or mutual benefit associations, but for a different reason. Employer-sponsored benefits were unstable because they were seen as gifts, not as promises.   As gifts, they were easily withdrawn.   Instead of formal benefit plans, employers followed a far more common practice and provided informal, and arbitrary, help to individual employees when they were disabled, sick or superannuated.   This informal system of cash payments were often bolstered by the practice of directly providing goods and services to employees.   This was the era of the company town where housing, stores and schools were provided by large employers.   Other companies provided less encompassing support such as employee cafeterias, recreational facilities, legal or mortgage aid.[11]   Direct provision of services, however, required investments of money, planning and administration on a scale that many firms were unable or unwilling to handle.   Thus many firms provided wages and nothing else.

This circumstance provided fertile ground for the development of insurance as an employee benefit.   Insurance plans allowed employers to provide relatively inexpensive and easily administered benefits to their employees.   Until 1911, insurance had been sold to individuals.   They underwent a physical examination, were assigned a risk and charged a premium.   But in

1911 the Montgomery-Ward Company approached several commercial life insurance companies to purchase life insurance policies for its employees. The purchase of insurance for a group was a dramatic break with custom for the insurance industry since Montgomery-Ward was proposing that its employees be insured under one policy without individual medical examinations. The underlying assumption was that the employees in poor health would be balanced out by the employees in good health yielding an average risk of claims on the policy. Most of the insurers dropped out of the negotiations when it became clear that a group policy could not be sold exactly as an individual policy, but the Equitable Assurance Society finally wrote the coverage in 1912. Despite opposition from smaller insurers and fraternal insurance societies, who were afraid that they would lose business, other large insurers such as Travelers and Aetna followed Equitable into the field. Life insurance as an employer-sponsored benefit plan soared. By 1917, 1,500 employers had adopted group life insurance plans, and by 1926 10 per cent of the workforce was covered.

Once commercial life insurance companies entered the group life insurance market, they quickly introduced this innovation into the accident and health (that is, sickness) insurance field. By 1919, group accident and health policies were being sold by all parts of the insurance industry. Before long it was extended still further into group annuities (i.e. pensions). The first group annuity policy was issued by Metropolitan Life in 1921, and employers began to fund pensions soon after. By 1924, 4 million employees were covered by approximately 400 pension plans. By the early 1920s all the basic types of employee benefits were in place, with the exception of health insurance, which did not develop until the 1930s.

The development of group insurance provided an efficient mechanism for employers to offer benefits to workers. However, other social developments were needed to provide the impetus for its adoption by large numbers of employers.

One major force was the development of an articulate social movement that came to be known as "welfare capitalism". This movement simultaneously encapsulated two of the basic, yet conflicting, impulses motivating employers to adopt employee benefits: the altruistic desire on the part of many employers to improve the living conditions of their workers, and the strong wish, on the part of employers generally, to eliminate the high labour turnover, routine sabotage and violent and costly strikes that had become the common reaction of many workers to the industrial conditions of the era.

In 1915 John D. Rockefeller Jr. promulgated a labour relations plan for his troubled Colorado mining company that brought into a formal programme varying employer activities that had been known for over 50 years as industrial welfare work. The plan involved several components: an employee representation council (known more commonly as a company union), new personnel management policies (such as reducing the arbitrary power of

foremen) and, most importantly for our purposes, employee
benefits. The employee-benefit component of the plan promoted
the building or funding of churches, schools and YMCAs for the
isolated mining communities owned or dominated by the company.
As the movement spread to Rockefeller-owned firms in more urban
areas, pensions, sickness benefits and life insurances were added
as means of controlling labour.[12]

Businessmen began to promote employee benefits and company
unions, both as humanitarian effor s to increase the financial
security of workers and as key el nts in a counter-attack to
trade union organising campaigns. It is difficult to disentangle
the motives, since both were there, but in some firms or
industries the worker pacification and control motive was
dominant. The welfare capitalism programme quickly spread
through major corporations, primarily into industries where trade
unions had been broken up in the previous decade. Moreover,
William Graham, the Equitable Life insurance company executive
who had developed group life insurance back in 1911, said that
employee benefits were "frankly a bid for co-operation from the
workers". Most employers felt that by cementing the loyalty of
workers to the firm through insurance, employers would weaken the
propensity of employees to unionise. Such programmes would also
have the effect of refurbishing the tarnished image given to "big
business" by the muck-raking journalists of the Progressive Era.

Not all companies embraced the entire Rockefeller plan.
Some firms established company unions while others were satisfied
with the adoption of some insurance benefits. Nevertheless, the
two phenomena - benefits and company unions - were often
intertwined. Employee benefits associations often served as the
basis for company unions, forming an already-existing
institutional base that could easily be transformed into
different functions. Company unions paved the way for employee
benefits in that they prepared employers to deal with workers in
new ways.

Throughout the 1920s, a difficult period for unions, welfare
capitalism and its employee benefits component spread across the
economy. The anti-labour impulses of employers were only part
of the factors that led to the spread of employer-sponsored
benefits. Several labour market trends as well as a number of
different government actions played a role as well.

During the First World War and for several years afterward,
employers faced a very tight labour market. Employers used
insurance benefits as a means to attract and retain scarce
workers. Insurance was attractive to workers and their
families; and, especially in the early days, it was available
from only a few employers. A survey in 1927 found that 129 of
430 firms responding said that the reduction of labour turnover
was a prime reason for the adoption of insurance benefits.
Employers were also quick to realise that benefits could be used
to further other personnel policies. Pensions in particular
were an excellent tool for the rejuvenation of a workforce: they

would allow an employer to retire old employees, who were thought to be less productive, and do so "without injustice".[13]

The removal of legal barriers to the development of group insurance and the establishment of new legal protections also enabled employer-sponsored benefits to gain a foothold. The reasonably extensive state regulatory system that was set up to protect the public from fraudulent insurance practices had to be altered to allow for group insurance policies to be sold. First, limits on the amount of insurance individual companies could sell had to be raised. Second, requirements for medical examinations had to be dropped. And third, new pricing methods had to be approved. In the five years after the 1911 introduction of the first group life insurance policy, state legislatures around the country removed these restrictions in response to employer demand and insurance company pressure.

Not only did legal barriers have to be dismantled, but legal protections that would give employers and unions incentives to support benefits had to be erected. Several changes in the federal tax codes achieved this goal. Before 1921 the interest from funds that an employer had put aside for employee pensions was taxable as income. Moreover, employees were taxed on the amount of money their employer put into the fund for their benefit. This left few incentives for employers to fund pensions or for employees to demand them. In 1921 the Internal Revenue Code was amended to remove these disincentives. Pension plan formation increased accordingly. The tax status of other employee benefits was not codified until 1953, but both before and after that date insured benefits were treated as business expenses for the employer and as tax-free income to the employee. This too encouraged the development of benefits.

Given these legislative and economic incentives, the growth of employer-sponsored benefits was further encouraged. By the late 1920s millions of workers were covered by some form of insurance benefits. The spread of benefits slowed rapidly due to the Depression, however. Preoccupied with survival and not welfare, employers ceased to expand their efforts to assure the financial security of workers through insurance and concentrated on keeping the companies alive. Welfare capitalism disappeared not to be revived until trade unions took up the banner of insured benefits during the Second World War.

The union response

Labour's response to employer-sponsored benefits passed through three stages: first active hostility, then competition and finally overwhelming demand. The initial union reaction to the imposition of employer benefits in the early 1900s was unfriendly. Union leaders saw that benefits were actual or potential anti-union tools. Moreover, union leaders felt that insurance was a cheaper substitute for wages. The American Federation of Labor Convention in 1924 went on record as complaining that workers often contributed in lower wages, many times the amount the employer actually spent on insurance for employees. In addition, unions believed that benefits represented a loss of the workers' freedom to spend wages as they chose.

Finally, unions objected to benefits, particularly pensions, because they decreased the mobility of workers. Workers, labour leaders argued, would be less free to leave a job if they would have to sacrifice their contributions to pension funds.

Insured benefits and pensions were clearly popular with workers, however. Unions could see this both by the response of their own members to union-sponsored benefits and by the requests of workers in non-unionised industries for benefits. By the 1920s many unions had overcome much of their ambivalence and had recognised the advantages of benefits; they now wanted to make sure that they controlled them. Ironically, some unions took the position that they wanted employees to pay for benefits, because this would strengthen union control over those benefits. In the end, unions were driven to co-operating with employers over benefits.

Collective bargaining over employee benefits took the form of union demands that employers participate in financing union benefits programmes. In 1917 the International Ladies Garment Workers' Union got the New York dress industry to agree to help fund the union's health centre. Six years later, the Amalgamated Clothing Workers successfully negotiated for employer contributions to the union's unemployment benefits fund.

In 1926, union and employer collective bargaining created the first insured sickness benefits plan to be purchased by an employer, when the Public Service Corporation of Newburgh, New York, agreed to provide insurance for its employees who were members of the Amalgamated Association of Street and Electric Railway Employees. Despite this breakthrough, collective bargaining over employee benefits moved slowly through the late 1920s and 1930s. Unions primarily were concerned with ensuring workers' financial security through public rather than private sector programmes (be they union or employer-sponsored plans). Throughout the 1930s and 1940s, the labour movement poured its energies into the drive for public old-age pensions and compulsory health insurance.

The explosion of benefits in the 1940s

By the 1940s both employers and unions still had mixed views on benefits. Many employers had created benefit plans by then, but a sizeable though dwindling proportion still remunerated employees solely with wages. One employer went so far as to argue that "giving sickness benefits in lieu of a wage increase was discrimination against the healthier employees".[14] Unions were ambivalent too. On the one hand, their members were increasingly in favour of benefits. For example, insured

workers showed extraordinary belief in insured benefits during
the Depression, when laid-off workers continued to return to
their old employers each month to pay their premiums.   Also
labour organisers for the Congress of Industrial Organisations
(CIO) continually encountered workers' fear that employer
benefits plans would be killed if the union was recognised as a
bargaining agent.   On the other hand, union officials were not
particularly in favour of benefits.   Union benefits had proven
an administrative and financial nightmare.   Unions were subject
to lawsuits by disaffected claimants for benefits;   they were
constantly forced to raise dues to cover rising costs;   and they
had to deal with occasional cases of fraud and the disappearance
of funds.   Trade unions constantly faced a choice between
improving member welfare, which required higher dues (and thus
led to fewer members), and building membership.

This welter of conflicting impulses and actions was
profoundly altered by the coming of the Second World War.
First, the war changed some of the balance between labour and
management.   What had been during the Depression an extremely
loose or overpopulated labour market became an extremely tight
market as much of the male population left the civilian labour
force.   Secondly, the war caused a shift away from production of
non-military goods to military material for the war effort.   The
combination of a tight labour market and a decrease in
non-military production created two major possibilities, economic
inflation and a wave of strikes.   These two possibilities were
the main reasons the Federal Government created the National War
Labor Board (NWLB) in 1942.   The creation of this Board was to
be the watershed event for the development of employee
benefits.   The NWLB was given the task of stabilising wages and
maintaining a steady economy.   Composed of representatives of
trade unions, corporations and the general public, the Board was
empowered to impose agreements between labour and management on
its own terms.   It quickly did so, establishing the "Little
Steel Formula" (named after a decision it made concerning the
smaller steel companies).   This formula limited wage increased
indefinitely to 15 per cent above the wage rates in effect in
January 1941.   Moreover, in 1943 the Board issued regulations
that employer contributions to insurance and pension plans that
were not in excess of 5 per cent of employee wages were not to be
included in the term "wages".   This meant that it was <u>outside</u>
the 15 per cent increase allowed in the Little Steel Formula.   A
member of the NWLB explained the rationale behind this second
policy: "The problem though was that we had to keep down
inflation.   So we agreed to allow increases in various benefits
that we felt would not be inflationary – vacations, insurance and
so on."[15]   After April 15 1943, when a Presidential Executive
Order tightened the flexibility of the Board, unions – and
sometimes management – sought hidden increases under the guise of
these "fringe adjustments".   Unions, scenting a way to secure
insurance benefits without paying the horrendous administrative
costs of operating these plans themselves, began to pressure and

18   6276d

then obtain, insurance and pension benefits. The Board would not order the inclusion of benefits in labour contracts at the behest of unions alone, but it did approve them when both labour and management agreed, or when a company voluntarily instituted a benefits plan. In short, the NWLB substantially aided the spread of employee benefits as an unintended consequence of its desire to regulate labour during wartime.

Other federal legislative enactments also encouraged the growth of fringe benefits. In 1940, Congress passed a tax on excess corporate profits which taxed 85-90 per cent of excess earnings. This law spurred corporations to set up welfare plans since such plans could come out of pre-tax income. Companies preferred to use profits to improve their labour relations rather than to pay the excess profit taxes. In 1942 the Internal Revenue Service (IRS) revised its regulations regarding employee benefit plans (Revenue Act of 1942, sections 165(a) and 23(p)). Employers were to meet certain requirements in order to have their pension plan obtain tax-exempt status, the chief one being that the plan must apply to a "reasonable percentage of the permanent employees" and must not discriminate in favour of highly paid workers. This change in the tax code had the effect of forcing corporations to expand their pension plans to larger numbers of employees. In addition, the IRS made the social insurance benefits tax-exempt, so that these too could be paid out of pre-tax corporate income. These various policy changes lowered the cost to employers of providing benefits. As a result, it became increasingly difficult for employers to refuse union demands for wage increases in the form of benefits.

By the end of the war, 6.7 million workers were covered by private sector pension plans, 32 million were covered by hospitalisation insurance and 12 million were covered by surgical group insurance.[16] This expansion in benefits constituted a major break with the past.

A number of forces converged to continue the wartime progress of benefit plans. First, the labour movement in a switch in strategy decided to push for reform on two fronts. In the mid- to late-1940s many of the major unions, particularly the Congress of Industrial Organisations (CIO), began to press for improved private sector employee benefit plans as well as for major public sector programmes, such as national health insurance. Unions had historically favoured government efforts to fill basic social needs. The labour movement had been the backbone of the drives for both national health insurance and social security pensions since the turn of the century, but by the mid-1940s many union leaders despaired of achieving effective public programmes. Thus, they began to press as well for employee benefits that would fill the same functions. Not only had the Government failed to institute desired social insurance programmes, but even the public social insurance programmes that had been achieved were not living up to their early promise. In the late 1940s social security benefits for retired workers averaged just US$29 per month, replacing about 20 per cent of the median wage. Faced with public programmes that provided benefits that were insufficient for workers' needs, unions resolved to obtain supplementary benefits from the private sector. Other labour leaders, particularly those in the CIO, felt that improved private sector benefits plans would pave the way to a public programme.

Unions from the Congress of Industrial Organisations spearheaded the campaign. These unions - the Autoworkers, Steelworkers and Mineworkers - were based in industries that had made some of the largest profits during the war. Having been organised later than those in other industries, many of these unions did not have their own benefits programmes (as did some of the older American Federation of Labor (AFL) craft unions. Moreover, these unions faced employers who were larger and thus more likely to be able to afford benefits plans. This campaign was given a boost when federal mediators, in the coal and the steel strikes of 1946 and 1949 respectively, sided with the unions and mandated some form of benefits.

The second force that consolidated the wartime gains was a number of federal decisions that provided the legal protection for their claims. The first and most famous decision came in the Inland Steel Case decided by the National Labor Relations Board (NRLB) in 1948. During 1946 and 1947 the steel industry began to take advantage of the loosening labour market to retire older workers by granting them pensions. The United Steelworkers protested, claiming that such a practice should be negotiated. The steel companies refused, arguing that pensions were not a negotiable item. This was part of a larger trend in the corporate community, where many employers during the late 1940s refused to allow their unilaterally developed benefits to be included in negotiated agreements. In 1948, the NLRB, later upheld by the Supreme Court, held that pensions were included in the term "wages and conditions of employment" in the Wagner and Taft-Hartley Acts. This meant that benefits had to be part of any negotiated agreement wherever a union represented employees. Two months later, in the W. W. Cross case, the NRLB expanded its ruling to insurance benefits, and one year later the Board ruled that employers could not institute a group insurance plan without consulting the union. The legal framework was, for the most part, now complete; benefits were installed as a permanent feature in labour-management relations.

Notes

[1] Charles Knight: "Fraternal life insurance", in Annals of the American Academy of Political and Social Science (Beverly Hills, California, Sage Publications Inc.), 1927, No. 130, pp. 97-102.

[2] Margaret Klem and Margaret McKiever: Management and union health and medical programs (Washington, DC, United States Public Health Service, 1953).

[3] Derek C. Bok and John T. Dunlop: Labor and the American community (New York, Simon and Schuster, 1970).

[4] William Greenough and Francis P. King: Pension plans and public policy (New York, Columbia University Press, 1976).

[5] United States Bureau of Labor Statistics: Beneficial activities of American trade unions (Washington, DC, 1928), Bulletin No. 465.

[6] ibid., p. 3.

[7] Nathaniel Minkoff: "Trade union welfare programs", in Union Health and Welfare Plans, 1947 (Washington, DC, United States Bureau of Labor Statistics), 1948, Bulletin No. 900.

[8] Helen Baker and Dorothy Dahl: Group health insurance and sickness benefits and collective bargaining (Princeton, New Jersey, Princeton University, Industrial Relations Section, 1945; Report No. 72).

[9] Richard Lester: Labor and industrial relations (New York, Macmillan, 1951).

[10] Louise W. Ilse: Group insurance and employee retirement plans (New York, Prentice-Hall, 1953).

[11] Stuart Brandes: American welfare capitalism, 1880-1940 (Chicago, University of Chicago Press, 1976).

[12] Irving Bernstein: The lean years: A history of the American worker, 1920-1933 (Baltimore, Maryland, Penguin Books, 1966).

[13] Albert Linton: "Life insurance companies and pension plans", in Annals of the American Academy of Political and Social Science (Beverly Hills, California, Sage Publications Inc.), 1927, No. 130, pp. 97-102.

[14] Baker and Dahl, op. cit.

[15] E. Robert Livernash: "Wages and benefits", in Woodrow Ginsburg et al. (ed.): A review of industrial relations research (Madison, Wisconsin, Industrial Relations Research Association), 1970, pp. 79-144.

[16] Health Insurance Association of America: Source Book of Health Insurance Data, 1981-82 (Washington, DC, 1981).

CHAPTER III

THE POST-WAR EXPANSION OF PRIVATE SECTOR SECURITY

The aggregate view

The era following the Second World War has seen the expansion of employee benefits from a scattering of uncoordinated employer- or union-sponsored plans into an extensive system of inventive mechanisms for protecting workers against numerous forms of financial insecurity. Once large numbers of both employers and unions realised the advantages of benefits plans during the wartime freeze on wages, much of the reluctance to create non-traditional forms of remuneration faded away. The inclusion of benefits into the legal framework guiding collective bargaining boosted this trend into a full-fledged transformation in the way workers are paid for their services. The statistics on the expansion of coverage make this clear. In 1939, just before the war, slightly over 5.6 million Americans were covered by hospitalisation insurance and 1.4 million had surgical insurance. By 1945, that 5.6 million had quadrupled to 24 million, while surgical insurance leapt to 8 million. And by 1950 hospitalisatiom insurance covered just under 60 million Americans, while surgical insurance coverage was at 39 million. Thus in ten years health insurance coverage had multiplied by 12 times. Pension coverage increased also during the same period, although not at the same rate as health insurance. In 1940, 4.1 million workers were covered by pension plans; in 1945, 6.4 million were covered and, by 1950, 2.8 million. Therefore, the number of Americans with the possibility of a pension at retirement in 1950 had more than doubled as compared with 1940.

In 1950, the Social Security Administration began to collect data on the number of employees covered by benefits plans. This data shows that coverage moved steadily upward. The rate of increase, however, changed as time went on. Many employee benefits expanded rapidly in the 1950s but the rate of increase slowed by the 1960s. The patterns of expansion differed between the various benefits. Between 1950 and 1955 hospitalisation coverage rose rapidly, increasing by 34.9 per cent; but by the 1970-75 per cent interval, coverage was increasing by only 9 per cent. This slow-down is not surprising, as much of the population was by then covered by hospital insurance. Pension plans followed a very different path. They too started quickly, increasing by 44 per cent between 1950 and 1955, but because pension plans started at a much lower point their growth has not slowed down to the same extent. Since 1960, they have steadily increased by approximately 16 per cent every year. Disability benefits have taken on yet another pattern. Temporary disability insurance (known historically as sickness benefits) was one of the earliest benefits to be developed. It covered a substantial number of workers by the end of the Second World War and has thus had a much smaller rate of increase.

By 1982, in the largest survey on benefits ever carried out by the United States Department of Labor, a large proportion of the American labour force had some employee benefits. Ninety-seven per cent of employees of medium and large firms had health insurance, 96 per cent had life insurance and 84 per cent had pensions.[1]

The number of employees that have been given benefits does not give us a sense of the full magnitude of the growth in benefits, however. One of the more outstanding aspects of the growth of corporate benefits plans has been the increase in the proportion of remuneration devoted to benefits rather than simple wages and salaries. In 1951, employers on the average paid 18.7 per cent of their payrolls for employee benefits. This proportion reached one-quarter of the payroll by 1963 and 37 per cent by 1980.[2] The increase in corporate expenditures for pensions and insurance benefits alone doubled in the last two decades, with employers devoting 5.1 per cent of remuneration to these benefits in 1966 and just under 9 per cent in 1977. The growth in employer expenditures for benefits has not been even across all benefits, however. Much of the increase can be tied to inflation in health insurance costs beginning in the late 1970s. Costs for pensions and other forms of insurance have risen steadily but not as steeply.

Unequal enthusiasm

Until now, the development of employee benefits has been pictured as a smooth progression, spreading to ever larger numbers of workers and their families, making up an ever larger proportion of employer labour costs, and looming as an ever larger issue in management and labour relations. But this is not the case. Not all firms offer the same benefits, or fund them with equal fiscal enthusiasm. Not all employees enjoy the same types or levels of benefits. There are decided differences in the insurance and pension benefits offered by different types of firms. The type of industry, size, location and degree of unionisation of firms powerfully affect the patterns of development of benefits. Moreover, within firms, the type and extent of employee benefits that an employee can command is affected by whether the worker is male or female, is paid by wages or salary or is a union member or not.

From the beginning, some types of industries have been able or willing to provide benefits earlier and to a greater extent than others. The most basic split is that between manufacturing and non-manufacturing sectors. Manufacturing firms have traditionally been more likely to offer benefits than non-manufacturing firms (such as retail stores, warehouses and hospitals). This is due in part to the fact that manufacturing firms are more likely to be unionised and/or are larger than non-manufacturing firms. This pattern has always existed, and even today continues, although the gap has diminished over time. The gap is particularly large in the case of pensions and sickness insurance and smaller in the case of health insurance (particularly major medical insurance). Employer expenditures for benefits also reflect industrial distinctions. In 1966, manufacturing industries devoted 6 per cent of employee remuneration to pension and insurance benefits, and non-manufacturing industries devoted 4.7 per cent. By 1977 manufacturing industries spent 10.9 per cent of their labour costs while non-manufacturing industries spent 7.9 per cent. In terms of dollars per work-hour, in 1966 manufacturers spent US$0.23 per hour versus US$0.15 per hour for non-manufacturing firms. In 1977 the gap was proportionately the same: US$0.94 versus US$0.62.

Unionisation is another major source of difference in patterns of benefit development (table 1). In general, employees in unionised firms are more likely to be covered by benefits.[3] But unionisation is a factor in and of itself. Unionised employees had more expensive benefits than non-unionised employees in the same firm.[4]

As may be seen from table 1, unionised establishments consistently spend approximately twice as much of their payrolls on benefits than do non-union firms. Moreover, the proportion of all employees covered is greater in unionised than in non-unionised firms. In 1979 larger proportions of unionised workers were covered by private pension plans than non-unionised workers.[5]

The provision of benefits also differs in relation to the size of firm. To begin, the larger the firm the larger the amount spent on fringe benefits. In 1959 firms with 500 or more employees spent 6.5 per cent of their payroll on fringe benefits, while firms with less than 100 employees spent 2.8 per cent of their payroll. The gap diminished over the next 25 years. By 1974, large firms spent 9.2 per cent of their payroll as opposed to 5.2 per cent in small firms. In addition, the larger the firm the greater the proportion of employees receiving benefits. A 1979 survey found that in firms with 500 or more workers 81 per cent of employees said that they were covered by retirement plans, while in firms with fewer than 100 employees only 34 per cent of employees said the same thing. Turning to health insurance, over 99 per cent of employees in firms with more than 1,000 workers reported health insurance benefits, but only 55 per cent reported the same in firms with 25 workers or less.[6] The geographic location of firms also appears to be a factor in differences in the development of benefits. Within industries regional differences were often striking. For example, in 1946 78 per cent of textile mills in New England offered some form of benefits while only 53 per cent of their south-eastern counterparts did so. All industries on the West Coast had lower rates for benefits, despite the generally higher wages. There is evidence that these differences still held true in 1980.

Table 1: Expenditures for non-office employee remuneration in unionised and non-unionised establishments: Selected employee benefits[1]

Year	Expenditures as a percentage of total worker remuneration			
	Unionised establishments		Non-unionised establishments	
	All industries	Manufacturing only	All industries	Manufacturing only
1959	...	5.8	...	3.3
1962	...	6.7	...	3.5
1966	6.3	6.5	2.5	3.6
1968	6.9	7.2	2.4	3.5
1970	7.7	8.4	3.1	4.2
1972	9.1	9.5	3.5	5.1
1974	10.0	10.2	3.8	5.4

... = figures not available.

[1] The benefits covered are voluntary life, accident and health insurance; retirement benefits; employer contributions to holidays with pay and supplemental unemployment insurance funds; savings and thrift plans; and severance pay.

Source: Based on publications of the United States Bureau of Labor Statistics.

The expansion of benefits to ever larger proportions of the labour force did not progress uniformly across all types of employees. Salaried versus hour workers, male versus female workers and Black versus White workers have different histories of obtaining eligibility for employee benefits. In part, these workers had different patterns because of their respective characteristics; in part, the patterns are a result of the fact that different types of people tend to cluster in different types of occupations and industries.

In the 1920s and 1930s, during the early years of employee benefits, employers often introduced benefits, particularly life insurance and pension benefits, to their salaried employees first. When it was clear that they were useful and affordable, or when the Federal Government mandated broad coverage, firms then enlarged their plans to include their wage (i.e. hourly) workers.[7] To this day salaried workers still get slightly better benefits. In 1977 employers spent 8.4 per cent of total remuneration on benefits for office employees and 7.8 per cent for non-office workers. In terms of expenditures on holidays with pay, pension plans and life, accident and health insurance, employers spent US$1.22 per hour worked by office employees and only US$0.76 per hour worked by non-office employees.

The disparity between salaried and hourly workers (broadly speaking, white- and blue-collar workers) has been minimised by several factors. First, blue-collar workers are more likely to be unionised than white-collar workers. Secondly, many benefits – including health, dental and accident insurance – are given out in equal amounts to all employees no matter what their means of remuneration. This is encouraged by the Internal Revenue Service whose regulations require that a reasonable proportion of the firm's employees be eligible for the benefit plan to obtain tax-exempt status. In addition, insurance industry practices require that 75 per cent of an employer's workforce be participants in a benefit plan in order to guard against adverse selection. This reduces the differences between various types of workers.

Through the years, men and women have differed in their access to employee benefits. Men and women have not always had equal rates of coverage. In 1969 a study found that 49 per cent of men, but only 21 per cent of women, were covered by pension plans.[8] In 1979, 55 per cent of all male workers were covered by pension plans in contrast to 40 per cent of all female workers. The evidence concerning the differences in health insurance coverage between men and women is mixed: two factors would seem to have led to this pattern. Early insurer rating (pricing) procedures for some types of insurance benefits stipulated that the rates were to go up for every 10 per cent increment in the number of female workers employed by the firm. This made insurance more expensive for employers with largely female workforces. The difference in receipt of benefits between men and women is also due to their different patterns of participation in the labour force. Women are clustered in low-paying and service industries which have generally been less likely to spend as much money on wages or benefits.[9]

The disparities between White and Black workers have not been documented as extensively, but a 1969 study found that among workers aged 58 to 63 White workers were more than twice as likely to have been covered by a retirement plan. By 1979 the gap had narrowed: 50 per cent of White workers were covered by a retirement plan while 46 per cent of "all other" workers had the same protection. Some of the reasons for the gap between Black and White workers are the same as those for the gap between male and female workers. Black workers also tend to cluster in certain industries and occupations.

When seen from this perspective, employee benefits begin to take on a more varied existence. While large sums of money are poured into private sector benefits and much of the American population is covered, employee benefits are much better for some Americans than for others.

Benefits adoption from the
perspective of individual firms

The description of the development of the context of employee benefits is based on the case histories of collective bargaining agreements reached by 32 organisations with a slightly larger number of trade unions. These case histories were collected under the Wage Chronology series begun by the Bureau of Labor Statistics in 1948, but the agreements reported often began as early as 1937. The firms concerned are listed in the Appendix.

When we trace the adoption of benefits by these 32 firms (which include public corporations), we soon find that, beneath the apparently smooth progression of benefits, there has been a much more staccato process. We can see this early in the adoption patterns of four major benefits: accident and sickness insurance, pensions, disability pensions and health insurance. A scattering of nine benefits plans were adopted by five firms in the pre-First World War period. Some of these plans seem to have been in the form of employee mutual benefits foundations. Then there was a lull, with only 12 plans (of various types) introduced by nine firms during the 1920s and 1930s. Benefits, as we would expect, expanded enormously in the wartime and post-war era. We find that one of the busiest years during this period was 1941, in which seven plans were introduced by five firms. It is noteworthy that this is two years before the NWLB began strictly to limit wages and to encourage the development of employee benefits as a substitute. In the decade following 1941 59 plans of various types were introduced by 26 firms. By 1951 these companies essentially had established their present benefits systems.

If we compare the development of various types of benefits, we can see that each took its own path. Of these four major benefits, accident and sickness benefits (that is, benefits replacing income lost due to sickness) were often the first benefit adopted by a firm. Accident and sickness benefit plans were introduced and peaked early (table 2). The first recorded plan in our sample was in 1902. Most firms adopted the benefit in the 1940s, and by the early 1950s three-quarters of them offered accident and sickness benefits. Eight firms (25 per cent of the sample) enacted accident and sickness benefits alone, but a somewhat more typical pattern involving ten firms was to do so in conjunction with another benefit: pensions (two firms), health insurance (seven firms), or health insurance and a disability plan (one firm). The later the adoption of accident

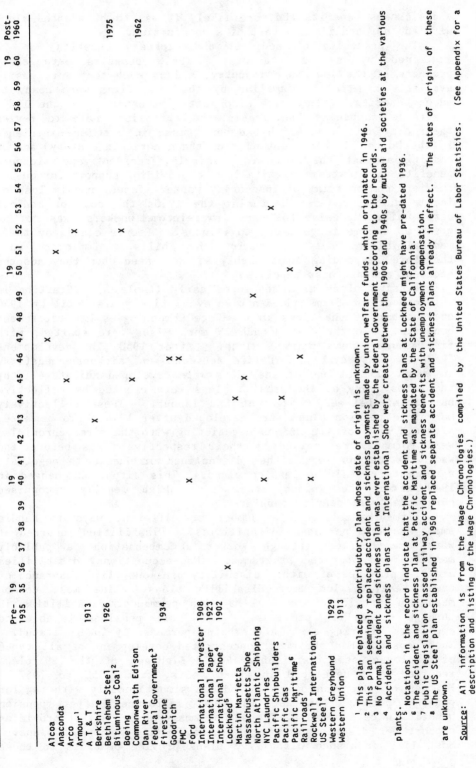

Company	Pre-1935	19 35	36	37	38	39	19 40	41	42	43	44	45	46	47	48	49	19 50	51	52	53	54	55	56	57	58	59	19 60	Post-1960
Alcoa																												
Anaconda																												
Arco														x														
Armour[1]	1913																											
A T & T																												
Berkshire																												
Bethlehem Steel[2]	1926																											
Bituminous Coal[2]																		x										1975
Boeing																												
Commonwealth Edison																			x									1962
Dan River												x																
Federal Government[3]										x																		
Firestone	1934						x																					
Goodrich																				x								
FMC													x															
Ford							x																					
International Harvester	1908																											
International Paper	1923																											
International Shoe[4]	1902																											
Lockheed[5]			x																									
Martin Marietta											x																	
Massachusetts Shoe												x																
North Atlantic Shipping							x								x													
NYC Laundries																												
Pacific Shipbuilders																x												
Pacific Gas											x						x											
Pacific Maritime[6]													x															
Railroads[7]																												
Rockwell International							x										x											
US Steel[8]																	x											
Western Greyhound	1929																											
Western Union	1913																											

[1] This plan replaced a contributory plan whose date of origin is unknown.
[2] This plan seemingly replaced accident and sickness payments made by union welfare funds, which originated in 1946.
[3] No formal accident and sickness plan was ever established by the Federal Government according to the records.
[4] Accident and sickness plans at International Shoe were created between the 1900s and 1940s by mutual aid societies at the various plants.
[5] Notations in the record indicate that the accident and sickness plans at Lockheed might have pre-dated 1936.
[6] The accident and sickness plan at Pacific Maritime was mandated by the State of California.
[7] Public legislation classed railway accident and sickness benefits with unemployment compensation.
[8] The US Steel plan established in 1950 replaced separate accident and sickness plans already in effect. The dates of origin of these are unknown.

Source: All information is from the Wage Chronologies compiled by the United States Bureau of Labor Statistics. (See Appendix for a description and listing of the Wage Chronologies.)

6276d

and sickness benefits the more likely it was to be adopted along with another benefit, as part of a combination.

The precocity of accident and sickness benefits can be explained by several factors. These benefits were early products of the insurance industry, and as such they were easily available and fairly familiar by the time firms were ready to adopt benefits. They were also getting cheaper. By the 1930s insurance companies had accumulated sufficient data to revise their original rates which had been based in part on experience in the United Kingdom (dating from the nineteenth century) and on hedging against the unknown. Thirdly, accident and sickness benefits were extremely suitable for providing support for one of the more common forms of insecurity workers faced, namely loss of income during illness. During the 1930s the cost of medical care, while expensive for many lower-income workers, was not as great as income forgone due to illness. People could pay their medical bills, but not their other bills. Employers were therefore responding to a highly visible need when they adopted accident and sickness benefits.

Pension plans also developed early (table 3). Starting in 1910 one or two firms added a plan every five years until by 1940 one-quarter of the firms in the Wage Chronologies had retirement benefits. In the next decade 15 more plans were started, with five plans added in 1950 alone. After 1950 plan development lessened considerably. Unlike accident and sickness benefits, in which all but one of the plans were developed unilaterally by the firms, many of the pension plans were created by collective bargaining between management and labour. These collectively bargained pension plans were developed after 1946. To be sure, although many of the unions negotiating with the firms chronicled were formally recognised by their respective firms before the war, the unions were either disinclined or unable to negotiate agreements containing pension plans. This situation changed in 1949 after the Inland Steel case which legally recognised bargaining over pension benefits.

Firms have chosen a number of different ways to handle employees with permanent disabilities. Disabilities incurred at work are handled through Workers' Compensation, a publicly mandated and operated programme. Non-occupational disabilities are the province of either disability pensions, life insurance or newer benefit, long-term disability plans. The most common means of providing for workers with permanent disabilities is through disability pensions. These are pensions payable to employees retiring early after being permanently incapacitated. Such pensions had the most concentrated development of all types of employee benefits (table 4). Eighteen of the 29 plans recorded were developed in seven years, from 1950 to 1957. Fifteen of the plans were introduced simultaneously with regular pension plans. Another 13 were introduced after pension benefits were adopted. The second most popular way of providing support for disabled workers is through life insurance plans. Most life insurance disability plans provide benefits to those

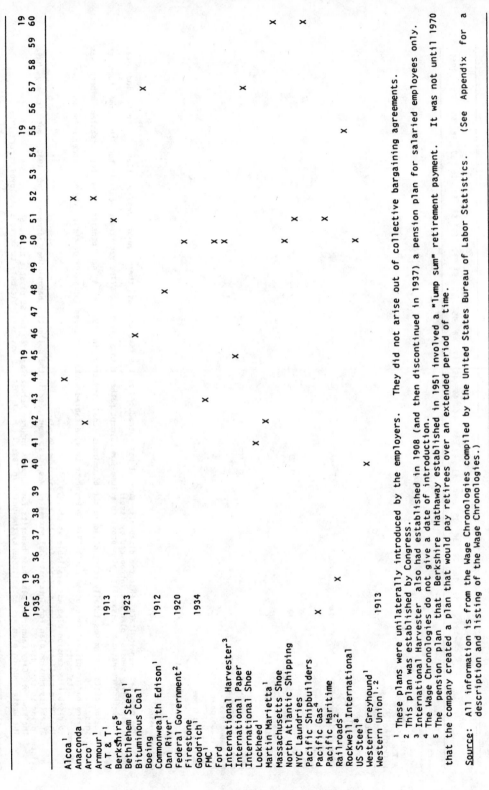

	Pre-1935	35	36	37	38	39	40	41	42	43	44	45	46	47	48	49	50	51	52	53	54	55	56	57	58	59	60
Alcoa[1]											X																
Anaconda																			X								
Arco[1]																			X								
Armour[1]	1913								X																		
A T & T[1]																		X									
Berkshire[5]																											
Bethlehem Steel[1]	1923																							X			
Bituminous Coal													X														
Boeing																							X				
Commonwealth Edison[1]	1912																										
Dan River[1]															X												
Federal Government[2]	1920																X										
Firestone																											
Goodrich[1]	1934									X																	
FMC[1]																	X										
Ford																	X										
International Harvester[3]																	X										
International Paper												X												X			
International Shoe																											
Lockheed[1]								X																			
Martin Marietta[1]									X																		
Massachusetts Shoe																											
North Atlantic Shipping																	X	X								X	
NYC Laundries																		X									
Pacific Gas[4]	X																										
Pacific Shipbuilders																		X								X	
Pacific Maritime																											
Railroads[2]		X																									
Rockwell International																						X					
US Steel[8]							X										X										
Western Greyhound[1]	1913																										
Western Union[1,2]	1913																										

1 These plans were unilaterally introduced by the employers. They did not arise out of collective bargaining agreements.
2 This plan was established by Congress.
3 International Harvester also had established in 1908 (and then discontinued in 1937) a pension plan for salaried employees only.
4 The Wage Chronologies do not give a date of introduction.
5 The pension plan that Berkshire Hathaway established in 1951 involved a "lump sum" retirement payment. It was not until 1970 that the company created a plan that would pay retirees over an extended period of time.

Source: All information is from the Wage Chronologies compiled by the United States Bureau of Labor Statistics. (See Appendix for a description and listing of the Wage Chronologies.)

Table 4: Timing of the introduction of disability pension plans by different firms[1]

Firm	Pre-1935	1935	1936	1937	1938	1939	1940	1941	1942	1943	1944	1945	1946	1947	1948	1949	1950	1951	1952	1953	1954	1955	1956	1957	1958	1959	1960	Post-1960
Alcoa																	X											
Anaconda																												
Arco																								X				
Armour							X																					
A T & T											+																	
Berkshire[2]																			+									
Bethlehem Steel[1]	+ 1923																											
Bituminous Coal[3]																												X 1966
Boeing[4]																												X 1974
Commonwealth Edison	X 1924																											
Dan River[5]																												
Federal Government[3]																									X			
Firestone																						X						
FMC[6]																							X					
Ford													+															
International Harvester[7]																	+											
International Paper																	+											
International Shoe																												X 1962
Lockheed																	+											
Martin Marietta																		X										
Massachusetts Shoe[5]																												
North Atlantic Shipping																		+										
NYC Laundries[8]																		X										
Pacific Shipbuilders[5]																												
Pacific Gas																			+									
Pacific Maritime																		X										
Railroads[7]			+																									
Rockwell International																				+								
US Steel																					X							
Western Greyhound	+																											
Western Union[9]	+ 1913																											

[1] The plus (+) sign indicates that the disability benefit was introduced at the same time as the regular pension plan. The X indicates that the disability pension plan was introduced by itself.
[2] The Berkshire-Hathaway disability plan provided a lump-sum payment rather than a pension. (The retirement benefits took the same form as well.)
[3] The benefits system was totally reorganised in the bituminous coal industry in 1974. A new pension plan for disabled miners was established.
[4] Boeing had no disability pension until 1974. Prior to this, disabled workers received the value of their life insurance, paid out over a set number of instalments.
[5] No disability pension plan was available as of 1979.
[6] The FMC disability plan was separate from the regular pension plan.
[7] Disability pension plan for International Harvester was first mentioned in the collective bargaining agreement of 1950, but it may have existed prior to this date.
[8] The New York City Laundries plan made benefits for workers injured between ages 60 and 65 payable at age 65.
[9] The Western Union plan was established by the Union in 1913. Until 1950, it was available only to workers employed before 1936.

Source: All information is from the Wage Chronologies compiled by the United States Bureau of Labor Statistics. (See Appendix for a description and listing of the Wage Chronologies.)

employees that are too young for retirement benefits, or serve as an alternative to disability pensions.   Only eight of the 32 firms had set up life insurance disability benefits as of 1980. Of those, two discontinued their benefits when they set up disability pensions.

Health insurance benefits were the last benefits to develop (table 5).   The earliest was in 1940, the last in 1960. Adoption by firms was concentrated into a relatively short length of time.   Of the 32 employees, 28 instituted health insurance plans between 1945 and 1955; moreover, one-half of these firms did so in half of that ten-year period.

Health insurance benefits were most often adopted by themselves;   18 of the 32 firms did so.   Another 11 adopted accident and sickness insurance at the same time as health insurance.   Thus, employers were simultaneously adopting benefits that covered both major forms of insecurity due to illness.

Despite their late development and thus the presence of trade unions, many health insurance plans were unilaterally adopted by management.   Of the 12 plans adopted before the 1949 National Labor Relations Board action requiring that insurance plans be collectively bargained, seven were the products of labour-management negotiations.   Thus, both in pensions and in health insurance, employee benefits continued to be installed unilaterally by management in spite of the existence of collective bargaining over wages with recognised unions.   Given these findings, we might tentatively draw the conclusion that until the Federal Government provided the legal support for including employee benefits in collective bargaining, companies were unwilling and unions were unable to place benefits on the bargaining table.

As we can see, each employee benefit has developed along a slightly different path.   Accident and sickness benefits and pension plans started earlier and were adopted over a long span of time.   Health insurance and disability pensions were much more concentrated in their development, with most plans appearing between 1940 and the early 1950s.

Given the wide variation in adoption patterns shown so far, can one say there are leaders and laggards?   Can we separate those firms who are generally among the first to choose to offer benefits from those who do so only when everyone else has already done so?   The answer is not clear.   Few firms were consistently leaders or consistently laggards.   There are a few patterns, however.   Several firms in the communications, transport and ship-repair industries (American Telephone and Telegraph, Western Union, Western Greyhound and the Bethlehem Steel Shipbuilding Department, respectively) developed benefits early on. Meanwhile, several West Coast firms and one textile firm were late developers.   Boeing, Pacific Coast Shipbuilding and Berkshire-Hathaway were still filling in their benefits combinations during the late 1950s and early 1960s, when most of

Table 5: Timing of the introduction of hospital and surgical insurance by differentfirms[1]

	1935	36	37	38	39	1940	41	42	43	44	1945	46	47	48	49	1950	51	52	53	54	1955	56	57	58	59	1960	61	62	63	64
Alcoa																														
Anaconda							X																							
Arco													X																	
Armour																														X
A T & T[2]																H	X S													
Berkshire								H																						
Bethlehem Steel											S	X																		
Bituminous Coal											X																			
Boeing[3]																		X												
Commonwealth Edison[4]						X																								
Dan River											S																X			
Federal Government							X				X																			
Firestone												X																		
Goodrich												X		S																
FMC																					X									
Ford[4]							X					X																		
International Harvester																			X											
International Paper															X															
International Shoe																H														
Lockheed[7]																														
Martin Marietta[4]									X	X																				
Massachusetts Shoe															X															
North Atlantic Shipping												H		S																
NYC Laundries										X																				
Pacific Shipbuilders																			X											
Pacific Gas[6]																X														
Pacific Maritime																H	S													
Railroads[5]																					X									
Rockwell International[4]							X																							
US Steel																H	S													
Western Greyhound[8]											X																			
Western Union																										X				

1 H = hospital; S = surgical. An X indicates that both plans were introduced at the same time.
2 A T & T introduced its major medical programme three years before its basic health insurance scheme. In 1960, A T & T introduced a "major medical" programme which paid hospital and surgery expenses in excess of the "local plan".
3 Boeing had previously a plan totally funded by the employees alone.
4 These plans were unilaterally introduced by these employers. They did not arise out of a collective bargaining agreement.
5 The date given - 1955 - was the date of consolidation of the "Hospital Association Plans" that various railways had established previously. Moreover, it was the date on which railways that had not offered such plans began to offer hospitalisation and surgical benefits to their employees. The Wage Chronologies for the railways do not give the date of introduction of the individual plans.
6 In 1944, Pacific Gas introduced surgical, medical and special hospital expenses plans. In 1948, the company introduced regular hospital insurance.
7 Lockheed had some form of insurance plan prior to 1949, but the Wage Chronologies do not make clear if it included hospitalisation benefits.
8 Western Greyhound did not begin contributing to the plan until 1956.

Source: All information is from the Wage Chronologies compiled by the United States Bureau of Labor Statistics. (See Appendix for a description –

the other firms had ceased their efforts, but on the whole few industrial differences appear at first glance.

The expansion of entitlements

The full significance of the development of employee benefits is revealed only when we become aware of the fact that these employer-sponsored programmes provide security for far more people than just their employees. Benefits have expanded to include both spouses and children of active workers and former employees (the retired, laid-off and disabled).

The reasons for the expansion of benefits to such individuals are not immediately clear. It would be logical to presume that employers would limit themselves to providing for those that added productive work to the firm. Dependants and former employees do not do this. They therefore have no obvious claims on the firm.

Yet, there were factors that led to the expansion of benefits to family members and non-active workers. One of the major forces behind the extension of benefits was the pressure by labour. Such an extension was urged as part of the union goal of helping workers provide financial security for themselves and their families. Unions found this task a bit easier than expected for several reasons. Achieving benefits for active workers alone would not ensure his or her financial security, given family demands and workers' needs after retirement. Also, unions sought company benefits as a substitute for non-existent public programmes. When federal health insurance programmes failed to pass through Congress in the late 1940s and social security benefits remained stalled, unions turned to the private sector. Insured benefits were falling in price during the 1950s. Employers could afford to extend benefits to dependants and former workers. Management did not need much pressure; employers recognised that extending coverage to dependants would lift financial burdens from the shoulders of their workers. Whether workers were distracted from work because of their own financial expenses or the expenses of dependants was immaterial. Employees valued benefits for both themselves and their dependants. Furthermore, insurance coverage for dependants fits in with management personnel goals. Benefits to dependants helped employers attract workers and retain them once hired.

As benefits expanded to those not directly employed by the firm, the definition of the proper rewards for work was transformed. Traditionally, wages were remuneration for a job that was performed. The amount of those wages was tied to the job and the contribution it made to overall productivity. The characteristics of the person who filled that job were irrelevant. No account was taken of family ties, obligations or future plans. Employee benefits, however, were decidedly different from wages. They acknowledged those circumstances and events that happened irrespective of an employee's type of job.

6276d

In offering insurance and retirement benefits to employees, employers in effect recognised their employees' out-of-work lives. This recognition led employers still further in the direction of providing security for those only peripherally attached to the firm. As the years wore on then, the values of benefits were extended to employees in varying relation to the firm as well as to their dependants.

The path of expansion of benefits came first to dependants, then to retirees and their survivors, and finally to laid-off workers. The high priority of dependants is not surprising. To the extent that employers use benefits in order to attract labour, reduce turnover and help their employees bear the brunt of sickness and old age, they are more likely to extend benefits to those their employees care the most about, their dependants.

As a consequence of the expansion to dependants, dependants soon vastly outnumbered the employees that were the initial objects of benefits. In 1954, for example, there were 1.3 dependant recipients of health insurance to every one worker recipient. By 1980, the ratio was 1.62 dependants to every one employee, according to the data provided by the Health Insurance Association of America.

The most common insurance benefits given to dependants are basic health insurance, major medical insurance, dental insurance and occasionally life insurance. In the majority of the Wage Chronologies (23 of 32), health insurance benefits were extended to dependants at the same time as to the workers. Of the remaining nine, three extended benefits to dependants in the next year or two, in order to guard against sudden costs. The six remaining firms - Alcoa, Berkshire-Hathaway, Ford, Massachusetts Shoe, New York City Laundries and Rockwell International - took an average of 15 years before they stretched their benefits to incude wives and children. Interestingly, three of these six firms were in declining industries and took the longest amount of time to extend benefits: Berkshire-Hathaway (textiles) allowed 29 years to elapse, Massachusetts Shoe 24 years, and New York City Laundries 12 to 14 years (first extending benefits to wives and then to children). Declining economic conditions cannot have been the reason for the tardiness of the other three firms, however, for they were in rapidly expanding industries: motor vehicles, electronics and aluminium, so we will have to look further for a complete explanation.

After dependants, employers next extended benefits to retired employees. Nineteen firms took this choice, two firms introduced the benefit to retirees before dependants, and five granted them simultaneously. The gap between retirees and dependants for those that did not introduce them simultaneously ranged from one year to 22 years with 6.3 years as the average length of time.

Pensions set the pattern for extending benefits to retirees. Once employers acknowledged a continuing tie to employees even after they had ceased to work, they found it easy to extend other benefits to retirees as well. Twenty-five firms extended health insurance, and 23 life insurance to their retired employees. Retired employees were most often granted health insurance benefits after dependants.

Life insurance was a benefit also commonly extended to retired workers. Again, such coverage was most often expanded to retirees after regular employees had already received the benefit. Most retirees began to receive these benefits in the 1950s, long after life insurance had been offered to active workers. Retirees usually receive lower benefits than active workers. It is unclear, however, whether this is because of employers' desires or because it is merely a practice imposed on them by insurance company policies (standard insurance principles require life insurance benefits to decline as the insured's age increases). Most life insurance coverage for retirees was lower than for active employees.

Beginning in the late 1950s, some firms extended benefits to laid-off employees, thus expanding the sense of obligation to former employees to those who had left the firm's employ for no reason of their own. The importance of the involuntary nature of a worker's discharge from work is highlighted by the contrasting treatment given workers on strike or who were fired or resigned. Sometimes firms have offered benefits that contained clauses that said that benefits were not applicable during periods of "unauthorised work stoppages".

The benefits most commonly extended to laid-off workers have been health, life, and occasionally accident and sickness insurance. Eighteen of the firms in the Wage Chronologies provide health insurance; 17 provide life insurance; and nine offer accident insurance. Providing benefits for laid-off employees is apparently more of an Eastern and mid-Western practice than a West Coast practice. Among the ten employers that gave no benefits to laid-off employees, four were West Coast firms. Of the nine firms that are located primarily on the West Coast, four offered no benefits to laid-off workers and another four only offered one benefit each. The amount of time laid-off employees have been entitled to benefits after lay-off has varied tremendously among the firms. Health insurance benefits have been available for periods ranging from seven days to years later. However, coverage was gradually expanded through successive labour agreements, until many of the firms now offering benefits to laid-off workers extend coverage from one to 24 months after lay-off.

Particularly in the 1950s, insurance was generally provided to laid-off employees so long as they kept up premium payments. Laid-off employees have expected to do so, even after active employees cease paying contributions towards premiums. Seniority, or years of service to the firm, is a common criterion for determining the length of time a laid-off worker is covered by insurance. Alcoa, for example, currently extends insurance for one year to employees with less than ten years of service and for two years to those with more than ten years of service. Ford, International Harvester and US Steel are also some of the firms that base their commitment to their laid-off employees on the length of time those workers have worked for the firm. Generally, the longer the coverage the more likely that laid-off employees have to pay the premiums.

With the expansion of benefits to individuals that were not current employees, company benefits emerged, whether intentionally or not, as a supplement to and even substitute for the welfare state. The inclusion of dependants and former employees enmeshed employers in the provision of social services. With this came questions about the costs and the consequences of attempting to provide suppport to a large proportion of the population. These questions were largely decided through decisions involving the content of benefits: the kinds of insecurity that would be mitigated, the amount of money or access that would be provided and the form in which benefits would be administered.

Notes

[1] United States Bureau of Labor Statistics: Employee benefits in medium and large firms, 1981 (Washington, DC, 1982), Bulletin No. 2140.

[2] Chamber of Commerce of the United States: Employee benefits 1980 and Employee benefits historical data: 1951-79 (Washington, DC, United States Chamber Survey Research Center, Economic Policy Division, 1981).

[3] Daniel Beller: "Coverage patterns of full-time employees under private retirement plans", in Social Security Bulletin (Washington, DC, United States Social Security Administration), 1981, No. 44, pp. 3-11.

[4] R.B. Freeman: The effect of trade unionism on fringe benefits (Cambridge, Massachusetts, National Bureau of Economic Research, 1978), Working Paper No. 292.

[5] Beller, op. cit.

[6] Amy Taylor and Walter Lawson: Employer and employee expenditures for private health insurance (Washington, DC, National Center for Health Services Research, 1981), Data Preview No. 7, National Health Care Expenditures Study.

[7] William Greenough and Francis P. King: Pension plans and public policy (New York, Columbia University Press, 1976).

[8] Gail Thomspon: "Pension coverage and benefits, 1972: Findings from the retirement history study", in Social Security Bulletin (Washington, DC, United States Social Security Administration), 1978, No. 41, pp. 3-17.

[9] Lauri Perman and Beth Stevens: Gender inequality and fringe benefits (New York University, Center for Applied Social Science Research, 1982), Reprint Series.

CHAPTER IV

BENEATH THE SURFACE: THE CONTENTS OF BENEFITS

Employee benefits remunerate for work, but they do so in a different way from wages. Wages have no strings attached; workers can spend them as they please. Benefits, however, cannot be spent by workers at any time for anything. Benefits have a content or meaning in addition to a price. To be sure, some benefits are like wages in that they involve actual money. Still, this money is only available under certain circumstances, such as when a worker becomes ill, too old to work or dies. Moreover, other benefits do not, strictly speaking, involve direct income. Rather, they provide access to various goods and services.

Because employee benefits provide support under strictly defined situations, employers and unions negotiate not only over the amount of money to be allocated to benefits but also over the specific types of benefits to provide and the circumstances in which employees gain access to those benefits. For the same expenditure of corporate funds, a number of different kinds of benefits can be purchased. The solutions to these issues that are agreed upon by labour and management reflect both the values and organisational interests of both sides. Consequently, each party must decide which instances of financial insecurity are worth protecting against, which catastrophes are more likely to occur, which circumstances are ones in which employers or workers can be held responsible, and what conditions should govern access to benefits. The values involve judgements concerning the contributions of different types of workers, the importance of the bonds between employer and employees and the value of the ties that bind workers to members of their families. These considerations underlie the rules governing eligibility and coverage and determine the distribution of benefits to some types of workers rather than others.

The current complicated system of insurance benefits, pension payments and payments in kind developed through a gradual process of accretion. Over the past 40 years, companies and trade unions have pieced together a complex system of policies on the basis of cumulative decisions. They have rarely reversed themselves, reducing benefits or shifting to a radically different system. Instead, policies were built up on the basis of what had been agreed upon in previous years. Thus the intricate set of rules, formulas and standards that are found today are based on a history of decisions.

This chapter will focus on two benefits: health insurance and retirement pensions. These two benefits were chosen for close analysis because they embody several of the aspects that crucially distinguish employee benefits from regular wages. Health insurance is the foremost example of the set of commonly provided insurance benefits that cover accident, dismemberment and death, because it demonstrates most strikingly certain qualities that all insured benefits have. Insured benefits are products that are designed, combined and sold by third parties, namely insurance companies. As such, these benefits are subject to a logic, practices and standards that are independent of labour relations considerations. Health insurance is not only a benefit, it is also the connection between the providers of a set of services and the market of consumers of those services. As a result it is often shaped by health care providers as much as by management and unions. Therefore, insurer and provider considerations are important to understanding the larger implications of using the private sector to provide security for workers.

Pensions are of equivalent interest, because they provide an example of another aspect of employee benefits. Pensions represent a long-term commitment by employers. Since most individuals live an average of 16.6 years after retirement at age 65, pensions can become a tie between employer and worker that often lasts for almost two decades. Pensions were chosen for study because they represent this protracted and major financial commitment for both employers and workers.

Health insurance

The present-day system

Health insurance currently is the second most prevalent private sector employee benefit, covering 97 per cent of full-time employees and 94 per cent of their dependants. The only benefit more widely available is holidays with pay; 99 per cent of full-time employees in industry in the private sector enjoyed such benefits in 1981. Furthermore, health insurance is one of the most popular benefits; 83 per cent of those with health insurance coverage in 1977 felt that health insurance was the most important benefit.[1] It is also a major force in the health care sector, responsible for reimbursing four-fifths of all hospital bills and half of all consumer expenditure for the services of physicians in 1980.[2] This coverage is expensive, particularly for employers. The average expenditure for employer-sponsored health insurance in 1977, for example, was US$775 per subscriber. On the average, employers paid three-quarters of that amount, with the employees assuming the rest.

Most benefits policies are organised into two distinct combinations — basic and major medical insurance. Basic insurance covers such hospitalisation, surgical and medical expenses such as hospital accommodation in a semi-private room, hospital care (meals, nursing, use of the operating room, medication, etc.), in hospital physician visits, sometimes home and office visits, and surgical fees. Major medical insurance was at one time a supplementary plan to basic insurance, but by now it has become a prominent part of health insurance. It covers those hospital bills that exceed the limits of a basic policy, as well as the broad spectrum of tests and treatments that comprise modern medical care: for example, radiological, physical and chemotherapy; in- and out-patient X-ray and laboratory tests; emergency care after accidents; the services of anaesthesiologists; blood transfusions; prosthetic devices; and ambulance transport. The services covered extend beyond those implied by a serious illness, however. Most leading policies now cover psychological testing, psychiatric care, convalescent care in a nursing home, haemodialysis, treatment for alcohol and drug abuse, and reimbursement for prescription drugs. Some firms have even added reimbursement for the expenses involved in the donation of an organ for transplant. In short, the most complete health insurance benefits programmes cover the most likely, and even some of the less likely, medical events encountered by employees.

Employer-sponsored health insurance comes in three basic forms: commercial insurance, Blue Cross/Blue Shield plans and independent plans (of which prepaid group practices known as health maintenance organisations, or HMOs, make up a large part). There are four major means by which insured persons are reimbursed, known as indemnity benefits, service benefits, independent or prepaid plans, and cost-sharing plans.

Commercial insurers have traditionally offered indemnity benefits; these benefits reimburse policy-holders (i.e. employees) on the basis of a fixed-fee schedule. Indemnity benefits paid by one Wage Chronology firm, for example, will pay US$80.00 per day for 365 days of hospital care and US$500.00 for performing an operation. This set amount is paid regardless of the actual cost. If the hospital rate or the surgical fee is higher, the patient must pay the remainder. If insurer fee schedules are maintained in parity with medical costs, the employee's benefit plan covers most of his or her medical bills. If the fee schedules fall behind, the employee receives less from his or her benefits. This problem is avoided by the reimbursement scheme developed and maintained by Blue Cross and, to some extent, Blue Shield plans.

The contribution of Blue Cross plans to health insurance reimbursement was the invention of service benefits. These policies, rather than reimbursing employees on the basis of a fixed list of prices, promise to cover the specified medical service, regardless of the cost. A Blue Cross hospitalisation policy will state that it will reimburse the employee for 70, 120 or 365 days in the hospital at the rate charged for a semi-private room. Thus, no matter what a particular hospital charges, the Blue Cross plan will pay the total bill. This lowers the likelihood that the employee will have to pay out-of-pocket expenses. Blue Cross and Blue Shield plans pioneered contract provisions that divided employees into two income groups. These insurers decreed that hospitals and physicians could not bill patients with incomes below a certain level for any sum beyond that reimbursed by the insurer. Hence, lower-income employees with Blue Cross/Blue Shield service benefits coverage have few out-of-pocket medical bills.

The third type of insurance plan, independent or prepaid plans, go even further than service benefits in reducing an employee's medical bills. A large proportion of independent plans are health maintenance organisations, which provide all medical care, from check-ups to major surgery, for a prepaid annual fee. In this instance, the employee does not have to pay anything out of his or her own pocket; as a result all medical expenses are reimbursed.

The fourth type of insurance payment mechanism is the newest and still most debated. Called cost-sharing, this type of policy, in contrast to other types of reimbursement schemes, pays for the bills incurred after a minimum amount has been paid by the employee. Insurers use two mechanisms, deductibles and co-insurance, to do this. Deductibles are set amounts, generally US$50 to $200, that must be paid by the employee before the insurance will reimburse any bills. Co-insurance takes up after the deductible has been met: here the insurer pays for some portion of the bill (currently the average is 80 per cent), while the patient pays the remaining portion. Sometimes insurers place an upper limit on the patient's liability. Cost-sharing is used in two ways. When this method is used instead of basic hospital, surgical and medical insurance, it is called "comprehensive insurance". These policies are only a minority of the group health insurance market, however. For the majority of policies, cost-sharing is restricted to the major medical policy that is used by most employers to supplement the basic hospital and surgical benefits.

As of the late 1970s, the 32 organisations in the Wage Chronologies have chosen all of these types of insurance plans. Several firms have plans that offer more than one type. In terms of hospital insurance (covering the most common and costly expenses), nine of the firms have indemnity policies, 20 have service benefit plans, one has its own clinic and hospital arrangement, and two offered two major choices: the Federal Government offers service and indemnity plans, while the Pacific Maritime Association (long-shoring) offers an HMO and a mixed service and indemnity plan.

While all 32 organisations provide health insurance plans to their employees, the plans are not identical in the value of benefits or in their impact on employees. The nine firms offering indemnity benefits have the greatest potential for leaving employees with out-of-pocket medical expenses (if the indemnity schedules are not revised with enough frequency to keep up with the high cost inflation in the health care sector, as has often been the case over the last 15 years). These benefits are

6276d

not as valuable to workers as the service benefits given by 20 other employers. Service benefits are most likely to cover bills. Moreover, employers providing indemnity policies are in effect promoting more regressive policies. The less that the insurance benefits cover medical bills, the more uneven is the impact of the benefit on different types of employees. Lower-income employees have to expend a larger proportion of their wages on medical care.

Before placing inappropriate emphasis on the more progressive nature of service benefits, it must be pointed out that many Blue Cross and Blue Shield plans have allowed their income limits on service benefits to lapse, thereby removing the stipulation that providers cannot charge patients for medical expenses beyond those reimbursed by the insurance company. Thus, some of the firms that offer service benefits to workers may not have health insurance benefits that are substantially better than indemnity benefits. The basic logic remains, however; those benefits policies that fail to cover medical bills are more regressive than those that do. As we can see, behind the glowing figure of 97 per cent of the population with health insurance coverage are differences in types of policies that create inequalities in the actual value of the coverage.

The development of health insurance
coverage of medical events

The US$200 semi-private room rates and the myriad of therapies, diagnostic tests and illnesses covered by today's complex financial reimbursement methods are a far cry from the health insurance benefits of the 1940s. In that decade, for example, the Commonwealth Edison Company of Chicago introduced a health insurance plan that provided, in total, US$4 per day for up to 70 days, US$100 per year for surgical fees and US$20 for miscellaneous hospital charges. The development of health insurance benefits from this meagre beginning to the abundance of coverage we find today is a story of insurance company initiatives, expanding entitlements and growing technologies.

Health insurance was still in its infancy when the firms in the Wage Chronologies began to construct their benefits programmes. It really began in 1932 with the organisation of the first Blue Cross plans and the beginning of insurance for hospital bills. This development was a distinct and controversial break from the past. Insurance, as defined in the traditional manner, is a pooling of financial resources to compensate for losses due to uncontrollable events that can wreak financial havoc on the victim. Events that were commonly insured were fires, floods and accidental death. Regular commercial insurance companies objected to insuring illnesses because it did not fit into the standard categories. It did not, they argued, involve large financial risks or occur in a completely unexpected or uncontrollable manner; much of illness is reasonably predictable and is partially under the control of the ill person. As a result, commercial insurers initially objected to Blue Cross plans and lagged behind in entering the market. Confronted, however, by the quick popularity of hospital insurance offered by Blue Cross, they had to swallow their objections. As a result, they too began to offer hospital insurance in the late 1930s. Their original attitude left a mark, however, in the types of medical bills that were deemed appropriate for insurance coverage. Insurers have always tended to cover the unexpected, the rare disease or condition, rather than yearly check-ups or voluntary (and hence controllable) surgery.

Commercial insurance companies in turn raised the stakes of competition in 1938 by introducing insurance for surgical fees. The non-profit plans created by physicians, known as Blue Shield plans, followed in 1939. In 1943, commercial insurers expanded once again and introduced medical visit insurance (for non-surgical physician services). And finally in 1949, major medical plans were developed by the private commercial insurers to complete the core of present-day health insurance benefits.

This chronology describes the development of health insurance as a product on a national market. It shows the choices available to those wishing to purchase insurance, but not the process by which firms and unions actually went about constructing the range of items of medical care coverage they would offer to workers. Only a coherent study of the development of benefits plans within a firm (or set of firms as we have here) can provide a specific history of the actual benefits that workers could use to pay for their medical care. So let us look at how individual combinations of employers and unions put together their benefit combinations. This process will be traced in terms of three central elements of health insurance benefits: the types of medical expenses covered; the reimbursement mechanisms determining the proportion of medical bills covered; and the requirements defining which employees and their dependants will qualify for specific parts of the benefits.

The firms represented in the Wage Chronologies built their health insurance combinations in sudden jumps rather than in year-by-year, step-by-step progression. Most firms started with a combination of minimal coverage of hospital and surgical expenses and of coverage of what was then known as "hospital extras" or "special services" (nursing, meals and the rent of operating rooms). Then, the firms often adopted a second cluster composed of physicians' insurance, maternity benefits, out-patient diagnostic services (such as X-ray and laboratory tests), emergency care and ambulance services. The third and last of the major waves of adoption consisted of the addition of major medical benefits, including coverage of psychiatric care, private nursing, purchase of blood products, and use of medical equipment. The remaining types of coverage for such services as anaesthesia, physical and radiation therapy and care of new-born babies were added in no particular order.

Several conclusions can be drawn from this progression. The first is that the development of health insurance as a benefit had definite structure. Firms did not add benefits in a random manner but followed a reasonably specific pattern. The particular pattern is a function of several factors. The primary one lies in the nature of health insurance itself. Health insurance is a product, which is developed and combined by outside parties and sold as a set of services. Many of the smaller types of services, such as coverage of diagnostic tests or treatments, were added in clusters because insurance companies grouped them together. They simply were not complex or expensive enough to necessitate a separate form of insurance. As such they were fitted into blocks depending upon their estimated costs. Specific combinations of services were combined depending upon the sum the clients had to spend. In short, this pattern is largely due to insurance company practices rather than to corporate or labour philosophy.

The expansion of benefits was also structured by the pace of progress in medical technology. The insurance of the 1940s, 1950s and even 1960s did not have to cover the use of computerised axial tomography (CAT) scanners, hyperbaric oxygen operating chambers or chemotherapy. Health insurance became progressively more complex as medical technology expanded.

And, finally, the development of health insurance benefits has been structured by the framework of labour-management relations. Benefits developed in waves in part because labour negotiations occurred every several years. Moreover, the give and take of negotiations created this pattern of stops and starts with small advances in random places. Minor fringe benefit changes, such as adding coverage for X-rays or ambulance transport, allowed management and labour negotiators to agree with each other on relatively inexpensive or administratively simple additions to benefits and yet gain credit with their respective supporters. Small additions to benefits can have more publicity value than actual value, in so far as employees want the protection but rarely need to avail themselves of the provisions. Management can quieten union demands without conceding large increases in labour costs, and labour union representatives can return to their membership with tangible advances that are not of a form that can easily be priced.

The second major conclusion we can draw from the study of the intra-firm development of benefits is that the development was in one direction: upward. Over the 40-odd years that the Wage Chronologies have been kept, there have been few reductions or roll backs in health insurance benefits. Counting all actions that might conceivably be defined as reductions, I found 28 possible reductions out of the thousand of benefit changes over the 40 years. Most of the reductions have been minor. In three instances the waiting periods for new employees to earn eligibility for coverage were raised by one, two or three months. In two cases benefits were reduced slightly or limited to a specific population: in 1948 New York City Laundries reduced the reimbursement for maternity care from US$57 to US$50; in 1978 the Federal Government lowered its maximum payment for alcohol, drug and psychiatric treatment from US$50,000 to US$20,000. In another three cases benefits were reduced in one aspect but increased in another, as when Firestone lowered the number of days the employee could be paid for hospital stays but increased the daily reimbursement rate. In five instances deductibles for either hospital care of physicians' fees and prescription drugs were raised slightly (by US$25 or US$50). The largest number of "reductions" involved the insertion of "co-ordination of benefits" clauses into the health insurance policies of 11 firms. These clauses stipulate that if the employee is covered by more than one policy (commonly the health insurance of a spouse) the two insurance policies will be co-ordinated so that the bill is paid only once. And finally over the years, only three benefits were formally eliminated. In short, by tracing the expansion of health insurance benefits, we can see that it was a process of accretion with few reductions and substitutions.

The proportion of funding devoted by employers to the provision of benefits has been some major reductions, however. As the Federal or State Governments have instituted social welfare programmes of their own, such as Medicare or state disability laws, employers have been quite content to reduce their role to providing supplementary benefits. This happened in the case of reduction in private health insurance for older workers over 65. The third major conclusion which emerges from the pattern of benefits adoption is that firms adopted insurance coverage for the most expensive and more visible medical occurrences first. Wage Chronology firms first adopted insurance to cover hospital bills and surgical fees, both increasingly necessary in the treatment of acute illness. They then added coverage for less central services – such as non-surgical physicians' bills and laboratory tests – as medical bills increased substantially. Finally, they put in benefits that employees were less likely to need or find expensive.

This progression represents the influence of two different philosophies on the proper role of health insurance as an employee benefit. Over the years two different philosophies have developed about the perennial problems of medical bills faced by workers and their families. One position argues that the major problem that workers face is the sudden onslaught of medical bills that follow a serious illness. This problem requires health insurance that covers the costs of such medical catastrophes. This is the traditional definition of insurance and is the approach advocated by insurance companies and employers. The other position, primarily taken by trade unions and consumer groups, argues that the primary problem most workers face is in paying for the more frequent visits to the doctor for the minor ills that occur before illness becomes serious. In contrast to medical catastrophes, this problem requires an insurance policy that covers small medical bills. This controversy has taken the form of a debate between those who favour "first dollar" coverage (coverage of medical expenses from the beginning of an illness) and those who support "last dollar" coverage (the coverage of medical expenses that amount up after long periods of sickness). Employers have long supported the purchase of "last dollar" coverage. They instigated the development of major medical insurance, which introduced the ideas of cost-sharing (namely co-insurance and deductibles) and coverage of catastrophic illness. Originally intended for upper-level salaried employees, major medical insurance soon spread to all employees.[3] Joined by the Industrial Relations Counsellors (an organisation of employer-oriented personnel officers that developed out of the welfare capitalism movement), employers pushed major medical insurance in order to discourage over-utilisation and unnecessary treatment. They hoped that it would give patients an incentive to insist on lower fees and thereby reduce costs. Major medical insurance also promised to reduce administrative costs. Major medical insurance also promised to reduce administrative costs because it would eliminate the payment of small claims. Unions on the other hand were strong proponents of "first dollar" coverage. They objected to the introduction of major medical coverage and ceased to object only when it became a supplement to basic insurance. Union representatives objected to the unequal burden "last dollar" coverage would place on low-income workers and argued that it would "relegate insurance to the minor role of standby protection against financial hardship".[4] Health insurance, in the unions' view, was to help maintain the health of workers, not merely to pay the expensive bills.

The health insurance structure we have today reflects the partial victory of both philosophies regarding health insurance. Coverage expanded in both directions. Employers achieved protection against catastrophes, with its deductibles and co-insurance, while unions were able to achieve "first dollar" coverage in basic insurance, low limits for the cost-sharing provisions and coverage of smaller expenses such as ambulance transport and out-patient testing. This compromise rested on two bases. The economic climate of the 1950s and early 1960s, with its rapid increase in both real wages and productivity, allowed employers to concede and unions to win a broad range of coverage.

The development of the content of health insurance benefits involves more than the expansion of coverage of different medical events. It also involves the development of new ways in which medical bills are reimbursed, whether through service benefits or indemnity benefits. The issue of the proportion of the medical bills that are reimbursed has raised a controversy similar to that between "first or last dollar" payment.

The type of reimbursement chosen has gradually shifted over the last 30-odd years. A majority of the companies in the Wage Chronologies (20 of the 32), first adopted indemnity benefits in their health insurance policies. These firms tended to be the first ones to introduce health insurance benefits. Since service benefits had already developed by the 1940s, this preference could not have rested on the unavailability of service benefits. Moreover, price does not seem to have been a major factor, because there is no clear evidence that indemnity benefits were any cheaper than service benefits. However, indemnity benefits were less risky to adopt in so far as they had specific financial limits.

Several clues as to the reasons why firms chose the less comprehensive indemnity benefits as a reimbursement may be found in a 1951 survey.[5] The employers surveyed disclosed that they chose indemnity benefits because they were primarily sold by commercial insurance companies. In the eyes of employers, commercial insurers had two advantages. First, they sold all types of insurance. This permitted employers to limit their personnel costs by purchasing their health insurance from the same supplier that provided their life, accident and sickness, and disability insurance. Secondly, commercial insurers provided policies that could be used nation-wide; this allowed an employer to offer coverage and negotiate with its union on a uniform, national basis.

On the other hand, indemnity benefits were clearly not the perfect solution as half of the 20 firms in the Wage Chronologies that orginally chose indemnity benefits switched to other types of benefits. Seven switched their benefits completely, going from indemnity to service benefits. Another firm switched to a comprehensive plan, and two added service-benefits insurance policies to their indemnity policies as choices for their employees. In contrast, not one firm switched from a service plan to an indemnity plan would mean a reduction in benefits. This finding is not surprising. Service benefits are more generous than indemnity benefits. They reimburse the entire cost of covered services rather than specified amounts of that service. Thus, transforming employee insurance from a service plan to an indemnity plan would mean a reduction in benefits.

The reasons for moving to service benefits were mixed. Switching to a service policy is a means of upgrading a benefits plan. Service benefits were also a favourite of progressive unions who saw them as one route towards more comprehensive medical care. Over the years, unions often have insisted on Blue Cross and Blue Shield plans in labour negotations.[6]

In recent years the trend towards service benefits has slowed. Instead, benefits plans have gone in two separate directions: towards the use of indemnity benefits as commercial insurers have overtaken the Blue Cross/Blue Shield plans in market share, and towards the provision of more comprehensive benefits through health maintenance organisations. Within the Wage Chronology firms, many organisations have offered HMOs as a choice for their workers. The future of reimbursement mechanisms for employee-sponsored health insurance benefits is cloudy, as the health policy experts grope for a solution to sky-rocketing health care costs.

As we have seen, health insurance has grown from the seemingly simple attempt by a group of consumers to pre-pay their medical care into an intricate financial system mediating the financial transactions between health care providers and consumers. Employers and unions have in part influenced that transformation and in part merely followed changing events. The substantive content of health insurance – the types of medical events covered and the proportion of the expenses reimbursed by the insurance – is a product of both these tendencies. Health insurance is a creation of the interaction between considerations of medical care and considerations of the interests of workers and employers.

Retirement plans

Pensions form a contrast to health insurance in a number of ways. Instead of offering a wide range of services, pensions simply come in the form of cash payments. As such, pensions have fewer strings attached than health insurance; workers may use them any way they please. In some ways, however, pensions still have many strings attached, more strings than any other benefit. Pensions require all sorts of conditions. Recipients must possess both certain personal attributes, such as age and a suitably long period of service with the firm. Pensions differ from health insurance in terms of their immediacy – they are only received by workers at the end of a reasonably long career; health insurance is available almost from the first day of work. Moreover, pensions are not as widespread as health insurance. To be sure, 84 per cent of workers in medium and large firms in 1981 worked in jobs covered by pension plans, but this large proportion is misleading, because the number of workers who actually receive benefits is much lower than the number of those who are covered. In 1980 the estimated ratio was 1 to 4: 9 million Americans were receiving pensions while 36 million employees worked in jobs that were covered by retirement plans.[7] So pensions have less immediacy than health insurance benefits in another way; they are less likely to be collected by workers. Whether this lack of certainty affects the value of pension plans in the eyes of employees is unclear.

Pensions also differ from health insurance in the social institutions that shape them. Pensions are not, for the most part, a product of outside institutions. The majority of retirement plans are devised, funded and distributed by firms or unions themselves. Insurance companies therefore play a less prominent role than with health insurance. On the other hand, pensions are strongly regulated by the Federal Government. All other benefits, while under the purview of the Departments of Labor and the Treasury, are minimally regulated. Only state departments of insurance have been given the task of overseeing the solvency of pensions.

The stakes involved in the content of pensions are high for employers, unions and the Federal Government because of the long-term requirements of service and funding, the large amounts of money involved and the impact of pensions on public policy. Pension benefits have thus been created in an atmosphere of conscious self-interest, ideological disagreements and deliberate strategy.

The present system

The private sector pension system is nothing if not diverse. American workers can currently earn one of several different types of private pensions: normal retirement benefits at age 65, early retirement benefits between ages 55 and 65 (depending on the firm or union) and disability retirements (which are often similar to early retirement pensions but are earned on a different basis). This discussion will emphasise normal retirement benefits, since they serve as the standard for the other two types of pensions. Normal retirement pensions are granted to employees under certain conditions. Unlike most other employee benefits, these conditions are specified by federal legislation. In 1976, Congress passed the Employee Retirement Income Security Act (known as ERISA), which set standards for every employer or union that voluntarily provides a retirement plan. Under this legislation, any employee is entitled to a Pension once she or he has worked for the employer for ten continuous years. This entitlement, the right to a benefit even if the employment relationship is terminated, is known as a "vested right". As an alternative, pension sponsors can set up "graduated vesting", which allows a worker a certain proportion of his or her ultimate pension for every year worked, starting with 10 per cent for five years of service and reaching 100 per cent by the fifteenth year of service. This option is available to employers who wish to raise the likelihood that their employees will earn at least part of a pension, since workers are more likely to be employed for five years than ten years. Vesting makes it possible for a worker to earn a pension without working for one employer an entire career. These federally mandated standards for vesting represent a triumph for those, particularly in the labour movement, who wanted to bolster workers' claims to retirement income after years of service to an employer. The issues surrounding the "rights" of workers to pensions will be discussed in a separate section.

The Employment Retirement Income Security Act does not specify the amount of money a pension must provide, but it does define two basic methods retirement-plan sponsors can use to compute pensions: "defined benefit" and "defined contribution" pension plans. Defined benefit plans are more common. Such plans provide either a specific amount (such as US$150 per month) or a clearly stated formula (such as a pension equivalent to 1.25 per cent of the average salary over the last five years the employee works) that will yield a specific monthly amount. Defined contribution plans promise that the plan's sponsor will contribute a certain amount for every year of employee eligibility (such as 1 per cent of salary). Under such a plan, the employee's eventual pension benefit is not exactly known, as it will depend on the amount contributed and the earnings on investment. One well-known defined contribution system is the Teachers Insurance and Annuity Association/College Retirement Equities Fund (otherwise known as TIAA/CREF). On the whole, however, this latter type of plan is becoming less popular.[8] It is still used for profit-sharing and savings or thrift plans. As of the late 1970s, 29 (90.7 per cent) of the Wage Chronology firms had defined benefit plans, and three (9.3 per cent of the firms) had defined contribution plans.

As with the health insurance reimbursement mechanisms, the choice of a formula for computing a pension benefit has subtle implications. Different pension formulas represent different options of the criteria by which employees should be granted income after retirement. Not surprisingly, these different criteria have varying effects on different types of workers.

The simplest formula for defined benefit plans is one that sets a flat amount per month for all workers, such as US$125 per month. This type of formula is geared towards equality of treatment and reward. It treats all employees in the same manner, ignoring all claims of higher salary, higher productivity, or longer service to the firm. As of the late 1970s, none of the Wage Chronology firms determined their pensions in this manner.

A second formula determines pension amounts by setting a specific amount to be multiplied by length of service. For example, Martin Marietta Aerospace, in 1976, paid US$9.50 per month for each year of credited service. Thus, an employee of Martin Marietta who retired at age 65 with 25 years of service, would receive a pension of US$237.50 per month. This formula has its own implicit values. It rewards workers on the basis of their loyalty to the firm and it ignores differences in earnings. One-half of the Wage Chronology firms use this method.

The third formula has become the most common among large firms, according to a recent Conference Board Report.[9] This method stresses earnings. Western Union, for example, pays a monthly pension benefit of 1 per cent of a worker's average annual pay during five consecutive years of highest earnings (which generally are the last five years before retirement). Here, workers are rewarded according to the character of their job in the firm. Once vesting is earned, it does not matter how long an employee has worked for the firm; length of service is largely not acknowledged. Some firms have mixed the latter two formulas to form a hybrid, which can be quite complicated. American Telephone and Telegraph, for example, pays 1.5 per cent of the average monthly wage for the highest five consecutive years of service times the last ten years of service after age 52, plus 1.125 per cent of average monthly wage for the highest five years of service times all remaining years of service. This last method is a compromise, rewarding workers for both the importance of their jobs to the firm and for their loyalty in the form of long service. It is also flexible, giving firms and unions a framework within which the emphasis can be shifted from one to another. The bulk of the remaining 13 Wage Chronology firms use this hybrid system. Finally, three firms have organised their retirement plans based on the defined contributions rather than defined benefits approach. In this situation firms use employee earnings for calculating company contributions.

These formulas have ramifications beyond the alternative acknowledgement of different aspects of the ties between an employer and his employees. Within one firm, the pension formula can affect different types of employees in different ways. If a firm uses the earnings-based formula, higher-salaried employees are more likely to receive higher pensions than under a seniority-based system. If the firm uses a seniority-based formula, lower-income employees, with little chance of upward mobility, would profit more. But this is not the entire story. For some of the firms, ten of them at the present time, the benefits formula is even more complicated and has even more ramifications on different types of workers. These firms, and many like them in the broader economy, purposely combine their private pension benefits with public sector social security benefits. They do this by subtracting some portion of the social security benefit from the amount arrived at, in the kinds of computations described above. Boeing Corporation, for example, offers a formula that takes 1.5 per cent of the highest five consecutive years of service and then subtracts 1.25 per cent of the social security benefit the worker would receive at age 65 multiplied by the number of years of service. By utilising this practice, known as "integration", employers deliberately structure their pension benefits so that they supplement the public sector retirement system. The goal behind the co-ordination of the two benefits is that, when combined, they will replace approximately 60 to 70 per cent of pre-retirement income, this being the standard common practice, on the assumption that expenses are less during retirement. The consequences of integration, however, are that the proportion of retirement income paid by the firm, and that paid by the Federal Government varies with different types of employees. Since social security benefits are designed to be progressive, they replace a larger portion of the income of the lower-salaried workers than of the more highly paid employees.

Once a firm integrates its pension formula with social security, this tendency is carried over to the private pension amount. The high social security benefit paid to lower-salaried employees takes up a larger part of their maximum allowable benefit as specified by the formula. As a result, the amount of money the firm must contribute is smaller. In short, private sector employers pay a smaller part of the total retirement income of lower-wage workers than they do for higher-salaried workers, if they choose to integrate their pension plans with social security. So firms choosing to integrate their pension formulas are in effect transferring the burden of providing retirement income for some of their workers over to the public sector.

One of the distinctive features of pensions as benefits is their high cost, and mechanisms needed to accumulate sufficient funds to pay pension obligations. Firms generally use one of three major mechanisms. They can fund and administer pension funds themselves, create a trust fund run by a bank or trust company, or fund pensions through insurance companies. These methods differ slightly in the amount of control that plan sponsors have over the investments of the funds.

Perhaps more than any of the other employee benefits, pensions have undergone a radical series of changes. Some of these changes were similar to changes in other insurance benefits and result from the invention of new technologies. In the case of benefits, this is translated into new financial mechanisms: new types of trusts, new forms of equities, new sources of funds. But these are minor in comparison to the changes in the very definition of the term "pension". These changing meanings in turn have affected the types of pensions provided, the rules governing who is eligible and the very formulas that determine the benefit amount.

The development of retirement plans

The content of pension benefits has always been both more simple than that of health insurance and yet at the same time infinitely more complex. Pensions still are - and always have been - paid out in money. They always have been - and still are - paid to a small number of categories of employees. The infinitely complex aspects of pensions are to be found more in funding, in the criteria that determine eligibility and in the formulas used to compute the final benefits.

The standards of eligibility

One of the key distinctions between wages and employee benefits, as previously argued, lies in the fact that benefits are given out only under specific conditions. Employers provide benefits to achieve certain goals. Whether they do so for more obvious personnel policy reasons, such as reducing labour turnover, or for more altruistic reasons, employers would like to ensure that the benefits reach those workers whom they would like to affect. As a result, they set clear eligibility standards for most benefits. Pensions are no exception to this tendency. In fact, pensions have more eligibility standards than perhaps all the other major benefits combined. These standards have eased considerably over the past 40 years, however.

The Wage Chronology firms represent two separate traditions. The first and numerically smaller group sets eligibility requirements of one to two years at most. Most of these were plans that required workers to contribute a proportion of their salaries in order to belong. Thus, it is not surprising that these firms allowed most workers to participate. The remaining two-thirds of the plans had a radically different approach. These plans introduced pensions plans with fairly stiff service requirements. Many of the firms initially required from 20 to 30 years of service before workers could obtain pensions. These standards gradually relaxed during the middle and late 1950s, so that by 1960 most firms had reduced their requirements to 15 years of service. By the mid-1960s, the standards had been reduced still further, to ten years.

Vesting, that is the granting of formal rights to a pension even after an employee has left a firm, was a concept that did not appear until the mid-1950s. Before this, the only firms that had provisions for vesting or "terminating" employees were those that had contributory plans. Those plans had provisions that allowed workers to withdraw their own contributions. During the 1950s, these firms began to add the interest earned on employee contributions to those withdrawals. As their versions of vesting, they began to permit those employees who had ten years of service to leave their contributions in the plan in exchange for a deferred benefit when they turned 65. Only one of the firms in the Wage Chronologies that had non-contributory plans, where employers pay all the cost, instituted vesting before 1955. With the exception of three firms, the remaining firms in the Wage Chronologies instituted vesting in a concentrated burst in the late 1950s and early 1960s. Most tied these original vesting provisions to age requirements. The bulk of those firms would not vest employees until they were at least 40 years of age, while a few would not do so until they were aged 50 or 55. Again, as we move toward the present day, these age requirements were reduced, and with the passage of the Employee Retirement Income Security Act (ERISA) in 1976 the minimum age for vesting dropped to 25.

Criteria for determining the amount
of benefits amounts

The most complex aspect of pension benefits is the formula for determining the amount of benefits. Unlike health insurance, there often are clear distinctions made in the pension benefits given to different employees. The general opinion that all employees should have equal access to medical care has not been matched by a view that all employees should receive equal pensions. Of all the major benefits, pensions have remained the closest to the concept of benefits as a reward for work rather than a social right. From the introduction of pension benefits to the present day, wide variations have been tolerated (or even encouraged) in the pension benefits provided to employees of the same firm.

The criteria yielding those differences have been quite varied, involving seniority, salary level and gender. Of the three, salary level and seniority have been the more important. Over the years, they have represented opposing approaches to the provision of retirement income i r superannuated employees. This division of approach has occu d as much within the labour movement as between labour and management. The Congress of Industrial Organisations (CIO) took the most radical approach to pensions. It supported what is now known as the "human depreciation" theory of pensions.[10] According to this theory, workers, like other factors of production such as machinery, depreciate over time and thus lose their value to the firm. As workers grow older, they no longer can contribute the same amount to the productivity of the firm and thus must be retired. Employers are financially obligated, in this theory, to make up in the form of pensions for the human energy that loyal workers have expended. As we can see, this argument contains the seeds of the belief that pension formulas should reward length of service to the firm: employees who have worked for more years, expending larger proportions of their strength and working lives, deserve larger pensions. Some members of the CIO even took a more drastic view of pensions, holding that pensions were the private sector's contribution to the overall task of supporting workers in retirement.[11] Pensions should supplement social security benefits and, in keeping with this, should be based on the same logic as social security, namely that all Americans are entitled to a minimum standard of living. As a result, the CIO pressured for pension formulas that offered generous base amounts or even the same amounts for everybody.

The American Federation of Labor (AFL) was more cautious in its claims for pensions. It held what is now termed the "deferred wages" theory of pensions.[12] This theory asserted that pensions were a form of remuneration for work performed that was simply being held until retirement. As such, pensions should be based on productivity, that is the worker's contribution to the firm. Here lies the rationale for pension formulas that are based on earnings rather than loyalty to the firm. This difference in view between the AFL and CIO was in keeping with the difference between the frequent exclusivism of AFL's craft unionism and the industrial unionism of the CIO, which emphasised downplaying differences between different categories of workers.

The AFL and CIO theories had an impact on the strategies they pursued in order to better the welfare of their members. The CIO, focusing on needs and general social welfare, treated pensions as supplements to the more crucial social security programme. In fact, CIO leaders acknowledged that the drive for private sector pensions was intended to pressure employers into supporting social security, if only to reduce their own labour costs.[13]   The American Federation of Labor leaders, holding on to their belief in pensions as only deferred wages, were more cautious about private pensions.   They were less inclined than CIO leaders to forgo wage increases in return for pensions. However, they too did go beyond the idea of pensions as merely a reward for work, for they insisted on minimum pensions in order to ensure that lower-paid workers would receive a pension.

Employers have never taken a firm stand on the exact definition of a pension.   Both the human depreciation and the deferred wage theories have a cost for the employer.   The human depreciation theory lays the moral and economic responsibility for providing income to retired employees right on the shoulders of employers.   It implies that employers are responsible for maintaining some minimal standard of living for workers as remuneration for using up their strength.   The Congress of Industrial Organisations leaders argued that contributory pensions were regressive, taking more from those employees least able to afford it.   Taken to its logical conclusion, the human depreciation theory would require some form of pension for every former employee; this would cost employers a lot.   The deferred wages theory is also costly to employers.   It seemingly is more conservative than the human depreciation theory in that it implies that pensions are merely enforced savings held by employers in trust.   But in actuality, it is equally radical in its premises.   The deferred wages theory implies that workers have a legal and moral right to pensions on the basis of productive work and not merely the less concrete notion of "service" used by the human depreciation theory.   The proposed link between work and pensions in this view is much more tangible and for that reason much more powerful.   While no employer has yet acceded to this idea, the Federal Government has implicitly endorsed the idea by passing legislation formalising the vesting rights of workers.[14]

An analysis of the history of benefits formulas, as preferred by the firms in the Wage Chronologies, mirrors the shifting definitions of what a pension is.   Quite common are alterations in the benefits formulas from an emphasis on seniority to one on salary and then back to seniority, or from a flat payment to one based on salary.   Fifteen of the 32 firms in the Wage Chronologies made at least one major change in their pension formulas between the 1940s and the present day.   The majority of the firms switched only once, however, and thereafter stayed with one type of formula.   Three of the organisations offered pensions that were based on the most radical of the pension definitions.   They provided pension benefits that gave the same flat amount to all employees.   These plans were all begun in the late 1940s or in 1951, at the height of the CIO campaign for pensions based on need.   Two of these firms, Ford and International Harvester, had created their pension plans in negotiations with the United Aerospace, Automobile and Agriculture Implement Workers (known more commonly as the UAW).

56

The UAW was one of the main forces behind the use of benefits as a tool of social reform. But as the UAW's philosophy changed to allow for more variation in pension benefits, Ford and International Harvester in 1955 switched their pension formulas to ones emphasising length of service as the key criterion for determining benefits amounts. However, in the late 1960s the two firms altered their formulas again, this time to a hybrid system taking both service and earnings into account. A third employer organisation, the Bituminous Coal Mine Operators' Association, negotiated their pension with the United Mine Workers, a union that had been a ferocious champion of private sector benefits. And, finally, the fourth plan was one dominated by the International Longshoremen's Association, an independent union affiliated with neither the AFL nor the CIO.

Fourteen of the 32 Wage Chronology firms based their pension formulas on earnings for most of the last 40 years. Most of these formulas were introduced either in the 1940s (or earlier) or in the 1960s. During the 1950s, formulas based on seniority were the pre-eminent method for computing benefits. We can see here a pendular movement in how pensions were viewed, with pensions first emphasising earnings as the criterion for computing retirement income, moving in the 1950s to seniority (or even social need) as a criterion, and then swinging back in the 1960s and 1970s to an emphasis on earnings.

The Wage Chronologies give no evidence that the difference between the AFL and the CIO in pension philosophy had an effect. Firms that negotiated with CIO unions were no more likely to compute their benefits on the basis of length of service (which is tied to the human depreciation theory advanced by the CIO). All told, the trend seems to be towards the view of pensions as deferred wages, and going into the 1970s the pension-formula changes were increasingly based on earnings. Whether this is a permanent trend is not yet apparent, however.

The third possible criterion for determining the amount of benefits over the years has been the gender of workers. Gender is often used as a distinguishing factor in such calculations, because women on the average live longer than men. Pension plans therefore must pay women for a longer period of time. As a result, the actuarial formulas that determine the amount of funding needed to maintain a pension plan have always forced employers to put aside larger amounts of money to fund pensions for their female employees. Insurance companies have generally charged 25 per cent more for annuity policies for women. The pension plans affected by this state of affairs are plans based on defined contributions. As may be recalled, employers under such plans guarantee that they will put aside a certain amount of money to purchase a retirement annuity, but they do not guarantee any specific amount. The eventual amount of the monthly benefit depends on the amount of money the employer has managed to collect and then used to buy a policy from an insurer. In this case, if firms put aside the same amount of money for their male and female employees, they will be forced to provide their female employees with an annuity of lesser value because annuities for women cost more money. Defined benefits plans, on the other hand, promise for example to pay 1 per cent of salary or US$49 per year worked. Unless they specifically make gender distinctions in their formulas, they are not forced to pay attention to gender differences.

None of the firms in the Wage Chronologies made distinctions based on gender in their pension plans. This criterion was simply not salient to the firms or the trade unions.

Notes

[1] Graham Staines and Robert Quinn: "American workers evaluate the quality of their jobs", in Monthly Labor Review (Washington, DC, Bureau of Labor Statistics), 1979, No. 98, pp. 3-12

[2] Robert M. Gibson and Daniel Waldo: "National health expenditures, 1980", in Health Care Financing Review (Baltimore, Maryland, Department of Health and Human Services), 1981, No. 3, pp. 1-54.

[3] Raymond Munts: Bargaining for health: Labor unions, health insurance and medical care (Madison, Wisconsin, University of Wisconsin Press, 1967).

[4] Jerome Pollack: "A labor view of health insurance", in Monthly Labor Review (Washington, DC, Bureau of Labor Statistics), 1958, No. 81, pp. 626-630.

[5] Jay Strong: Employee benefits plans in operation (Washington, DC, Bureau of National Affairs, 1951).

[6] Munts, op. cit.

[7] Alicia Munnell: The economics of private pensions (Washington, DC, The Brookings Institution, 1982).

[8] Mitchell Meyer: Profile of employee benefits: 1981 edition (New York, The Conference Board, 1981), Report No. 813.

[9] Meyer, op. cit.

[10] Charles Dearing: Industrial pensions (Washington, DC, The Brookings Institution, 1954).

[11] Paul S.J. Harbrecht: Pension funds and economic power (New York, The Twentieth Century Fund, 1959).

[12] Harbrecht, op. cit.

[13] Dearing, op. cit.; Richard Lester: Labor and industrial relations (New York, Macmillan, 1951).

[14] Dennis Logue: Legislative influence on corporate pension plans (Washington, DC, American Enterprise Institute, 1979).

CHAPTER V

CONCLUSIONS

For the vast majority of Americans in 1940, remuneration for a job well done consisted of cash in a pay envelope. By 1980, that envelope contained more than just cash; it also contained a list of explanations, descriptions of holidays with pay earned, contributions to a savings plan, deductions for health and dental insurance, and so forth. The intervening 40 years have seen the development of a varied collection of privileges, protections and cash remunerations that enormously changed the way people are rewarded for work. This set of employee benefits, as they are now called, also represented the private sector's attempt to protect the welfare of workers and their families through insurance and savings programmes that mitigate the adverse effects of life events such as illness, old age and death.

This mixed system of rewards and rights did not develop overnight. Nor did it develop along any kind of predictable path. Benefits grew out of a series of compromises, serendipitous choices and public policy incentives. There were several different possible responses to the needs of workers. Employer-sponsored benefits plans are merely the most successful solution out of a set of possible responses.

Over the past century, a variety of social groups have attempted to provide protection against insecurity. Ethnic groups, community associations and charitable fraternal societies have all provided various forms of insurance and small cash payments to help their members replace the income lost due to sickness, retirement or the death of a wage earner. Most of these programmes have long ago been relegated to a minor role, however. They were never able to overcome several inherent limitations. First, most of these societies could not sustain a sufficiently large membership to provide low-cost benefits. In order for groups to do so, they must be able to spread the costs of such protection over a large number of people. Most of these organisations, as local organisations, were not able to do so. Their benefits either remained small in order to keep dues down or they offered generous benefits at a price that kept their membership low. Moreover, these groups were voluntary organisations; very often the provision of benefits was their primary activity. Thus, members could easily withdraw when the costs became too high. Those members that remained were often the ones who called the most upon the services of the organisation. As a result, the benefits became even more costly as they were being used more often with even fewer members.

Organisations based in the workplace partially avoided some of these problems. They could reach and attract a sufficient membership more easily. Moreover, their major activities were in areas other than social welfare benefits. Thus, members were part of the organisation irrespective of the cost of benefits. Membership was much more stable. This is not necessarily a mandate for employer-sponsored benefits programmes, however. Both union-sponsored or jointly administered programmes were equivalently suitable from this perspective. These two latter solutions never became a major alternative, however.

Both union and jointly managed benefits programmes, while filling the necessary qualities presented above, had problems of their own. Union-sponsored plans suffered from the fact that they were both a building-block and a drain on the union. Even though benefits attracted members, they also forced up union dues and drained funds away from other union activities such as organising or supporting strike actions. The combination of positive and negative aspects created sufficient ambivalence about union benefits to lead many unions to avoid benefits programmes altogether.

The major problem encountered by union programmes, however, was one of inauspicious timing. Union-sponsored benefits programmes were consolidating their initial successes when they ran into the strong anti-labour drive of the 1920s and the Depression of the 1930s. By the time the Depression ended, unions were preoccupied with rebuilding membership, obtaining wage increases, and only then offering benefits. During the 1940s, unions seeking a solution to the perennial problems of funding benefits programmes attempted to negotiate employer contributions to union-run plans. The 1947 Taft-Hartley Act forbade this type of organisation, so unions were forced back into either developing their own programmes with their own limited resources or sharing the credit for benefits with employers.

By this time some employers had begun to provide benefits on their own. Employers were finding that benefits helped their workers, discouraged unionisation and lowered labour turnover. The advantages were sufficient for large employers to begin to construct small benefits programmes. This mixed situation of some employers, some union and some jointly sponsored benefits might have continued were it not for several federal government actions. The best known was the ruling by the National War Labor Board that benefits did not come under the wage freeze imposed during the Second World War. This encouraged employers and unions to negotiate for benefits in place of wages. Federal tax laws in 1942 and 1954 provided an economic incentive for employers to sponsor benefits plans by giving certain tax incentives for this purpose. Finally, the Supreme Court and the National Labor Relations Board ruled in the late 1940s that employers could not simply refuse to negotiate over benefits. With these actions, the legal framework for the development of benefits was established.

The impact was quite clear. Employer-sponsored plans thrived. They were helped on their way in part because unions realised that, as long as a strong union influence was maintained through the collective bargaining process, such programmes could improve the security of union members. The ultimate success of employer-sponsored plans, then, was due to the fact that they fitted the needs of employers and trade unions and attracted the support of federal policy-makers.

Unlike federal social welfare programmes, where the policy-making functions are centralised, employee benefits programmes have developed separately within each firm or industrial association. The result has been an uneven process of development, with bursts of activity and then lulls. Each benefit has had a separate pattern of adoption. The simpler benefits, such as accident and sickness or life insurance, were introduced first. They were benefits composed by insurance companies and thus easy to install. They also met some of the more pressing needs of workers at the time: to provide income when the wage earner was ill or to tide his widow over if he died. The more complicated benefits were adopted later. Health insurance and disability plans arrived in a rush, during the period from the mid-1940s to the mid-1950s. Pensions followed their own idiosyncratic pattern. Some firms instituted pensions as early as the turn of the century, while some did so as late as the 1960s, but most firms instituted pensions in the early 1950s, after the great union drive for pensions in the late 1940s.

The benefits adoption process has been uneven in yet another way as well. Firms interlaced the adoption of new benefits for their active employees with the extension of their existing benefits to workers' dependants and to former employees. Benefits were first extended to dependants, then to retirees and finally to laid-off employees. This pattern of adoption illustrates the values underlying the private sector development of pensions. Benefits were initially "extended" to different categories of individuals on the basis of their contribution to the productive life of the organisation. Employers were willing to provide active employees with benefits because this would attract workers and reduce turnover. Subsequently, firms extended benefits to the dependants of workers on the grounds that the expenses incurred by family members were as much a burden on workers as the workers' own expenses. Since these burdens might affect the workers' ability to work, benefits were in the interest of the firm. In effect, firms gave benefits to dependants in order to keep them from being distractions to workers. This is evidenced by the fact that, unless they could prove dependancy, spouses of female workers were not given benefits as early as the spouses of male workers.

Retired workers could not make the claim that they were even related by proxy to the productive life of the firm. They were merely former workers and the extension of benefits to this group was one more step away from the use of benefits as direct remuneration. Here benefits became a reward for past service. The extension to laid-off workers altered the meaning of benefits still further; benefits were now a service and employers provided them because the major means of access was through the workplace.

The development of benefits through the 1970s was uniformly upward. Various firms and unions proceeded at different paces but all did so along the same general path. No one reduced benefits. At worse, firms postponed adoption of new benefits or improvements in existing benefits. Atrophy, not elimination, was the pattern when firms needed to call a halt to benefits expenditures.

No firms were clear leaders or laggards in benefits adoption over the entire 40 years or for all types of benefits. Those firms that adopted benefits later than the majority of firms tended to meet the existing standards once they decided to offer benefits. In other words, laggards would adopt several benefits at once in order to catch up with the others. Moreover, they would set their benefits at a level near the centre of the distribution. Thus, laggards would spend large amounts of funds to bring themselves quickly up to the point that the leading firms had already reached over a longer period of time.

This is not to imply, however, that benefits levels are consistent across different firms. The Wage Chronologies have shown us that beneath the figures of coverage for the entire national labour force, there are major differences in the types and value of benefits offered to workers. Some firms – in communications, transport and public utilities – typically developed benefits before other firms. Others – primarily those located on the West Coast – tended to adopt benefits late. The firms in the service and textile industries were often the last to institute a benefit.

Employers can control the extensiveness of their benefits in three major ways. They can cover greater or fewer numbers of catastrophic events, set up narrow or broad standards of eligibility or manipulate the criteria that determine the final benefit amount to be given out to each individual. Employers and unions can adjust health insurance benefits by providing insurance that covers either a broad range of medical occurrences or limits itself to the less common catastrophic events. They can choose insurance with more or less comprehensive reimbursement mechanisms, so that employees pay greater out-of-pocket expenses. The less comprehensive the payment scheme, the cheaper the insurance is to the employer. Retirement policies can be manipulated by restricting the types of pensions offered. Firms with minimal benefits combinations, for example, limit their retirement policies to those that have reached the age of 65 or fail to offer disability pensions.

A more subtle method for controlling employee benefits is to structure eligibility rules to include or exclude employees and dependants. Employers manipulate eligibility rules for different benefits in varying ways. The eligibility rules guiding the qualification for health insurance benefits are rarely used to restrict access. Health insurance as an employee benefit seems to have brought with it the general American value that lack of money should not be a bar to receiving health care. There has been only one major exception to this open-handedness. During the first ten to 15 years of the provision of health insurance benefits, lower benefits were provided to dependants and retired employees. Both of these groups were heavy utilisers of medical care; as a result their insurance coverage was more expensive than that covering regular employees. This has been the only substantial limit placed on access to health insurance benefits over the past four decades.

Pensions are not distributed with such even-handedness. Most firms originally established substantial age and/or service requirements for pension benefits. Over the years these standards have dropped and pensions have become more accessible. Firms now, with federal standards to guide them, provide pensions to employees who have worked for the firm for at least ten years. Many employees still fail to meet such requirements, and so in that sense pensions are still the least accessible of the benefits.

The final mechanism for managing benefits is the use of benefits formulas to provide larger or smaller amounts of benefits. Most health insurance benefits policies are given out without regard to seniority or salary. The only exception has been the use of service benefits that guarantee that lower-income workers will have low or non-existent out-of-pocket medical costs. This is quite different from pension plans. Pension formulas make clear distinctions between workers on the basis of salary or seniority. These distinctions are embedded in the very definitions of pensions.

All of these manipulations have varying effects of different levels on employees within a firm. Some ways of structuring benefits are regressive, with lower-income employees either bearing higher costs or receiving lower benefits than they would under other formulas. Other ways are progressive, with benefits either minimising income differences between different employees or actually providing higher benefits for lower-level workers. The provision of coverage for catastrophes, with its cost-sharing mechanisms, is one example of a regressive practice. The use of seniority-based pension formulas rather than earnings-based formulas is the opposite.

The future of employee benefits is not clear. Much depends on the resolution of a number of issues that surround this hybrid social institution. As we have seen, the linkage of social welfare benefits to the rewards for work has had several implications. First, benefits often are, and have been, distributed on the basis of private sector values of length of service and productive contribution to the firm rather than according to need or political right, as it would be within the public sector. Secondly, the kinds and levels of benefits often vary among different parts of the private sector, as different

6276d

employers and unions have varying resources to provide such benefits. This has both positive and negative aspects as it both ensures flexibility and capacity to tailor benefits to specific situations, and provides widely uneven benefits based on the industry or firm where an individual finds employment, not on his skills or occcupation. Third, benefits are often established in the context of negotiation between two opposing sides, each with its own strategies for providing worker security. This can provide an open exchange of ideas and a mutual testing of proposals, but it also can result in trade-offs based on issues unrelated to benefits. The ramifications of each of these aspects of private sector employee benefits must be explored before we can make a decision about how we would like our society to distribute welfare benefits.

As we have seen, employee benefits have changed considerably over the past 40 years, growing increasingly complex, more accessible and more universal. As they have done this, they have moved away from the status of mere alternative forms of remuneration and closer to the status of being a general social welfare system. The expansion to dependants and former employees (even laid-off workers) shows the extent to which the general population depends on some form of tie to the workplace, not the Government, for basic forms of protection against financial insecurity.

As benefits have moved towards the status of a substitute or supplement to public programmes, they have increasingly come under scrutiny by the public sector. The entire tenor of government regulation of employee benefits has changed over this period. State and federal agencies initially limited themselves to the function of ensuring that benefits plans were not fraudulent, i.e. that they remained solvent and delivered what they promised. There was little concern for the content of those promises. Government interest in benefits quickened when it became clear that benefits could be used as a tool in the maintenance of labour peace. First, the Government encouraged benefits in order to reduce the pressure on its own wage-freeze policies; and then it acknowledged their continued usefulness by mandating that they be fodder for collective bargaining. But as benefits grew in scope and coverage of the population, they began to be seen as alternatives to or adjuncts of public programmes, to be manipulated by government in the interests of social policy. As a result, employee benefits have come under closer inspection and the very provision of benefits policies have now been subject to federal intervention. With the passage of the Health Maintenance Organisations Act in 1973 (which mandated that employers offer the choice of a health maintenance organisation to its employees), and the Employee Retirement Income Security Act in 1976 (which set specific standards for pension eligibility regulations), the Federal Government firmly declared benefits to be in the realm of public policy.

Whether benefits continue to straddle the line between being a reward and a right is an open question. Various forces have combined to create a private sector welfare system. This coalition is composed of parties with ever-changing and at times divergent interests. Its future survival seems to rest on its continued satisfaction of public needs and private interests.

FIRMS AND UNIONS CONTAINED IN WAGE CHRONOLOGIES
AND THEIR STANDARD INDUSTRIAL CLASSIFICATION (SIC)

1. Aluminium Company of America (Alcoa)

    Major activity: Aluminium processing and mining
    SIC Code: 33
    Union: United Steelworkers of America; Aluminium Workers
      International Union

    Source of Wage Chronology: United States Bureau of Labor
      Statistics, Bulletin No. 1815; Supplement to Bulletin
      No. 1815 (Apr. 1980).

2. Anaconda Company (Montana Mining Division)

    Major Activity: Non-ferrous (copper) mining and processing
    SIC Code: 10
    Union: United Steelworkers of America

    Source of Wage Chronology: United States Bureau of Labor
      Statistics, Bulletin No. 1953; Supplement to Bulletin
      No. 1953 (Mar. 1979).

3. Atlantic Richfield Company (formerly the Sinclair Oil
    Facilities)

    Major Activity: Petroleum pipelines and refining
    SIC Code: 29
    Union: Oil, Chemical and Atomic Workers International
      Union

    Source of Wage Chronology: United States Bureau of Labor
      Statistics, Bulletin No. 1915; Supplement to Bulletin
      No. 1915 (Nov. 1977).

4. Armour and Company

    Major activity: Meat processing
    SIC Code: 20
    Union: Amalgamated Meat Cutters and Butcher Workmen

    Source of Wage Chronology: United States Bureau of Labor
      Statistics, Bulletin No. 1682; Supplement to Bulletin
      No. 1682 (Feb. 1979).

5. American Telephone and Telegraph Company (A T & T) – Long Lines Deparment.

   Major activity: Communications
   SIC Code: 48
   Union: Communications Workers of America

   Source of Wage Chronology: United States Bureau of Labor Statistics, Bulletin No. 1812; Supplement to Bulletin No. 1812 (May 1976).

6. Berkshire–Hathaway Incorporated

   Major activity: textile manufacture (fabric)
   SIC Code: 22
   Union: Amalgamated Clothing and Textile Workers' Union

   Source of Wage Chronology: United States Bureau of Labor Statistics, Bulletin No. 2061 (May 1980).

7. Bethlehem Steel Corporation (Shipbuilding Department)

   Major activity: Shipbuilding and repair
   SIC Code: 37
   Union: Industrial Union of Marine and Shipbuilding of America

   Source of Wage Chronology: United States Bureau of Labor Statistics, Bulletin No. 1866; Supplement to Bulletin No. 1866 (Jan. 1977).

8. Bituminous Coal Mine Operators

   Major activity: Coalmining
   SIC Code: 12
   Union: United Mine Workers (UMW)

   Source of Wage Chronology: United States Bureau of Labor Statistics, Bulletin No. 2062 (Nov. 1980).

9. The Boeing Company (Washington Plants)

   Major activity: Transportation equipment; defence
   SIC Code: 37
   Union: International Association of Machinists and Aerospace Workers

   Source of Wage Chronology: United States Bureau of Labor Statistics, Bulletin No. 1895; Supplement to Bulletin No. 1895 (Feb. 1979).

10. Commonwealth Edison Company of Chicago

   Major activity: Electric utility
   SIC Code: 49
   Union: International Brotherhood of Electrical Workers

   Source of Wage Chronology: United States Bureau of Labor
   Statistics, Bulletin No. 1808; Supplement to Bulletin
   No. 1808 (June 1978).

11. Dan River Incorporated

   Major activity: Textiles
   SIC Code: 22
   Union: United Textile Workers of America

   Source of Wage Chronology: United States Bureau of Labor
   Statistics, Bulletin No. 2048 (Mar. 1980).

12. Federal Employees Under the General Pay System

   Major activity: Public administration
   SIC Code: n.a.
   Union: n.a.

   Source of Wage Chronology: United States Bureau of Labor
   Statistics, Bulletin No. 1870; Supplement to Bulletin
   No. 1870 (Sep. 1980).

13. Firestone Tire and Rubber Company
   B.F. Goodrich Company

   Major Activity: tyres and rubber products; chemicals
   SIC code: 30, 28
   Union: United Rubber, Cork, Linoleum and Plastic Workers
   of America

   Source of Wage Chronology: United States Bureau of Labor
   Statistics,
   Bulletin No. 2011 (Aug. 1979).

14. FMC Corporation - Chemical Group (Fiber Division)

   Major activity: Chemicals (rayon yarns and fibres)
   SIC Code: 28
   Union: Amalgamated Clothing and Textile Workers' Union

   Source of Wage Chronology: United States Bureau of Labor
   Statistics, Bulletin No. 1924; Supplement to Bulletin
   No. 1924 (Mar. 1979).

15. Ford Motor Company

   Major activity: Transportation equipment; automobiles
   SIC Code: 37
   Union: United Automobile, Aerospace and Agricultural
     Implement Workers of America (UAW)

   Source of Wage Chronology: United States Bureau of Labor
     Statistics, Bulletin No. 1781; Bulletin No. 1994.

16. International Harvester Company

   Major activity: Agricultural and construction equipment
   SIC Code: 35
   Union: UAW (see Ford Company for full title)

   Source of Wage Chronology: United States Bureau of Labor
     Statistics, Bulletin No. 1887; Supplement to Bulletin
     No. 1887 (June 1979).

17. International Paper Company (Multiple Mill Group)

   Major activity: Paper manufacturing
   SIC Code: 26
   Union: United Papermakers International Union;
     International Brotherhood of Electrical Workers

   Source of Wage Chronology: United States Bureau of Labor
     Statistics, Bulletin No. 2023 (Sep. 1979).

18. International Shoe Company

   Major activity: Footwear manufacture
   SIC Code: 31
   Union: United Shoe Workers' of America (USW); Boot and
     Shoe Workers' Union (BSW)

   Source of Wage Chronology: United States Bureau of Labor
     Statistics, Bulletin No. 2010 (July 1979).

19. Lockheed – California Company

   Major activity: Aircraft manufacture; weapons manufacture
   SIC Code: 37
   Union: International Association of Machinists and
     Aerospace Workers

   Source of Wage Chronology: United States Bureau of Labor
     Statistics, Bulletin No. 1904; Supplement to Bulletin
     No. 1904 (Feb. 1979).

20. Martin Marietta Aerospace

   Major activity: Missile (defence) manufacture
   SIC Code: 37
   Union: UAW (see Ford Company for full title)

   Source of Wage Chronology: United States Bureau of Labor
      Statistics, Bulletin No. 1884; Supplement to Bulletin
      No. 1884 (Sep. 1977).

21. Massachusetts Shoe Manufacturers

   Major activity: Women's footwear manufacture
   SIC Code: 31
   Union: United Shoe Workers (USW)

   Source of Wage Chronology: United States Bureau of Labor
      Statistics, Bulletin No. 1993 (1978).

22. North Atlantic Shipping Association

   Major Activity: Longshore operations
   SIC Code: 44
   Union: International Longshoremen's Association (ILA)

   Source of Wage Chronology: United States Bureau of Labor
      Statistics, Bulletin No. 2063 (June 1980).

23. New York City Area Laundries

   Major activity: Commercial laundering
   SIC Code: 72
   Union: Amalgamated Service and Allied Industries Joint
      Board (affiliated with Amalgamated Clothing and Textiles
      Workers' Union)

   Source of Wage Chronology: United States Bureau of Labor
      Statistics, Bulletin No. 1845; Supplement to Bulletin
      No. 1845 (Oct. 1977).

24. Pacific Coast Shipbuilders

   Major activity: Shipbuilding
   SIC Code: 37
   Union: Pacific Coast Metal Trades District Council (which
      represents a coalition of AFL crafts unions)

   Source of Wage Chronology: United States Bureau of Labor
      Statistics, Bulletin No. 1982; Supplement to Bulletin
      No. 1982 (Feb. 1981).

25. Pacific Gas and Electric Company

> Major activity: Electric utility
> SIC Code: 44
> Union: International Brotherhood of Electrical Workers
>
> Source of Wage Chronology: United States Bureau of Labor
> Statistics, Bulletin No. 1761; Supplement to Bulletin
> No. 1761 (Apr. 1979).

26. Pacific Maritime Association

> Major activity: Longshore operations
> SIC Code: 44
> Union: International Longshoremen's and Warehousemen's
> Union
>
> Source of Wage Chronology: United States Bureau of Labor
> Statistics, Bulletin No. 1960; Supplement to Bulletin
> No. 1960 (May 1980).

27. Railroads - National Railway Labor Conference

> Major activity: Railroad transportation
> SIC Code: 40
> Union: Non-operating Employees - a coalition of unions
> organised along craft lines called the Railway Labor
> Executives' Association (RLEA)
>
> Source of Wage Chronology: United States Bureau of Labor
> Statistics, Bulletin No. 2041 (May 1980).

28. Rockwell International Corporation

> Major activity: Electronics, aircraft, space systems
> manufacture
> SIC Code: 36, 37
> Union: UAW (see Ford entry for full title)
>
> Source of Wage Chronology: United States Bureau of Labor
> Statistics, Bulletin No. 1983; Supplement to Bulletin
> No. 1983 (Feb. 1981).

29. US Steel Corporation

    Major activity: Steel manufacture
    SIC Code: 33
    Union: United Steelworkers of America

    Source of Wage Chronology: United States Bureau of Labor
      Statistics, Bulletin No. 1814; Supplement to Bulletin
      No. 1814 (July 1980).

30. Western Greyhound Lines

    Major activity: Transportation
    SIC Code: 41
    Union: Amalgamated Transit Union; International
      Association of Machinists and Aerospace Workers

    Source of Wage Chronology: United States Bureau of Labor
      Statistics, Bulletin No. 1595; Supplement to Bulletin
      No. 1595 (May 1978).

31. Western Union Telegraph Company

    Major activity: Communications
    SIC Code: 48
    Union: Communications Workers of America; United
      Telegraph Workers

    Source of Wage Chronology: United States Bureau of Labor
      Statistics, Bulletin No. 1927; Supplement to Bulletin
      No. 1927 (Aug. 1978).